COMPANION PLANTING

A detailed guide to organic gardening, including sheet
composting techniques and making the most of mutually
beneficial plants.

COMPANION PLANTING
SUCCESSFUL GARDENING THE ORGANIC WAY

by

GERTRUD FRANCK

Translated from the German by
Transcript

THORSONS PUBLISHING GROUP

First published in Germany as
Gesunder Garten durch Mischkultur
© 1980 Südwest Verlag GmbH & Co. KG, München
First published in Great Britain April 1983

British Library Cataloguing in Publication Data

Franck, Gertrud
Companion planting: successful gardening the
organic way.
1. Organic gardening
I. Title   II. Gesunder Garten durch
Mischkultur, *English*
635'.0484   SB453.5

ISBN 0-7225-0695-3
ISBN 0-7225-0694-5 Pbk

Published by Thorsons Publishers Limited,
Wellingborough, Northamptonshire, NN8 2RQ, England.

Printed in Great Britain by Woolnough Bookbinding Limited,
Irthlingborough, Northamptonshire.

5   7   9   11   13   15   14   12   10   8   6

Contents

To my children and grandchildren.

I have no theories.
I just have something to show.
I show the facts,
and something about the facts
that has been too little seen or not at all.
Those who will listen to me, I take by the hand
and lead them to the window.
I push the window open
and point to what is outside.
Martin Buber

Introduction

The system of gardening presented in words and pictures in this book, is based on more than thirty years of observation and practical experience. It all began when we noticed some rather puzzling facts which recurred year after year and finally produced the conviction that certain plants will thrive in some plant communities but not in others. This led to regular experimentation, which included such matters as the right way to till the soil.

Our garden's main purpose was to provide healthy food for a large household of people and animals, so we were preoccupied, not only with finding the best way to keep the garden free from diseases and pests, but with seeing how to restore it each year to tiptop condition. One clear though unexpected result was that culinary herbs not only form a vital food supplement but actually stimulate the growth of other crops. The insights gained over a period of time and repeatedly checked and compared with what happens in nature, had now to be incorporated in a horticultural system: the observed interrelationships of plants and the ideal cycle of development and decomposition above and below ground had to be tested and elaborated.

A companion-planted garden as described here, with appropriate measures for preserving soil fertility by mulching and composting, and with the suitable pre-sowing, secondary sowing and re-sowing of short-lived plants, has been proved over many years to be a viable proposition. What we have done is to copy Nature, in which no bare, uncolonized soil goes to waste. As a bonus, this method makes a significant contribution to energy conservation: no foreign substances requiring energy for their manufacture and transport need be brought into our gardens. The companion-planted garden described here exists on its own resources.

The Fundamental Ideas

Most people are familiar with the term 'organic gardening', especially if they have anything to do with agriculture or horticulture and the production of safe foodstuffs. The expression is admittedly inexact but everyone knows what it means. Generally speaking, by 'organic' we understand a form of gardening which does not rely on poisons to control pests, diseases and weeds and does not use artificial fertilizers; its purpose is to avoid deleterious influences of any sort. Nevertheless, traditional methods of tilling the ground are often still employed. The soil is turned in the usual garden beds and manure is dug into it. What is more, there is often heavy manuring of a specific nature, appropriate only to the needs of the plant population growing in the beds that particular year. Treatment of this type with mineral fertilizers can disturb the steady rhythm in the life of the soil. In this way, organic gardening, although it does not use poisons, fails to take advantage of all the pure, high-quality nutrients available from natural sources. In view of the danger to which the environment is exposed nowadays, gardeners must surely be asking themselves to what extent they must adopt a positive approach in their work and abandon a negative one. Fortunately, our own researches will supply an answer to this question.

If we are to garden in a way that will be helpful to the environment, we shall have to radically reorientate our activities whether we are working in the vegetable patch or in the orchard. Not only this, but we should try to cultivate beautiful and well laid out gardens, full of glorious colours and delicate scents which are a source of strength and joy.

The garden is inhabited by an animal world which can live there in accordance with the laws of nature. All creatures are more or less useful to us when we know their living conditions and take these into account; even the 'pests' are useful as indicators of our omissions or mistakes. These are not the only factors that enter into organic (and trouble-free) gardening and need careful consideration. It is true that the gardener is not a party to the dumping of industrial waste on the environment or to the pollution of air and water, but he or she should endeavour to utilize all garden and household refuse as far as possible for keeping the land fertile without outside help.

Pests and plant diseases are not just things to be fought with the help of chemicals; they point to faults in cultivation and ought to be regarded in that light. Given the opportunity, the garden itself will achieve a balance between the conflicting interests of its plants and animals, its microflora and microfauna. Chemical control uses up our energy resources and is an unnecessary burden on the environment. By adopting sensible preventive measures of plant protection, the gardener who works organically leaves no polluted water behind him and, thanks to his special mode of cultivation, actually saves water instead of pouring it down the drain.

The buying of garden accessories should be minimal. Simply by utilizing plant growth and energy from the sun, the gardener can prepare a soil in which micro-organisms will flourish, this being a prerequisite for the growth of the higher plants. He or she will also seek to promote a healthy cycle between soil and plants by returning everything that grows in the garden to the soil as an active fertilizer assisting future growth. In this way, crops will be assured and yields will be high. Two things are essential: learning to see connections and the absorption of sensible, reliable knowledge.

1.

The Vegetable Garden Throughout the Year

For this type of garden, the pattern to follow is unspoilt Nature, which displays an extravagant mixture of vegetation in woodland, field and meadow. All the plants grow together in dependence on one another, and each plant community exists in harmony with its environment and is not interchangeable with any other community. Plant life is enormously varied, and comprises trees, shrubs, herbs, cultivated plants and wild flowers of all sorts. It also has an active association with large and small animals living in the same area; these leave their droppings there, die there, and their decomposing bodies maintain the life of the soil and supply nourishment to the plants. Neither monoculture nor patches of bare soil unclothed with vegetation are to be found in Nature, which constantly reveals how processes of transformation occur and how organic materials are broken down.

Repeated observations have led to thinking along new lines and, finally, to a type of gardening which may be called 'fully organic'. The many processes so clearly visible in Nature have been carefully analyzed, referred to the garden and its needs, and then formulated as the simple, practical instructions set out in the following chapters.

It was problems associated with the proper feeding of people and animals which gave the initial impetus towards devising an organic horticulture. Evaluation of all observations plus many tests carried out over a long period have led to a system and plan that can easily be put into practice in every garden. Planting is done in such a way that, at any given time, the environment is positive for the partnered plants. They act as good and protective neighbours, and help to ward off pests and diseases from one another. The treatment of diseased plants and the application of pesticides to kill off certain insects is of no concern in the companion planting method. This type of cultivation is concerned with which plants will respond well to a certain environment, and in which environments pests can be discouraged and diseases prevented. The choice of environment requires thought: it has to possess those positive features which will bring out the best in our plants and those negative ones which will inhibit whatever would exploit their weaknesses.

Row-crop Cultivation
To be explicit, compatible plants are described in later sections, account being taken of the very important questions of their patterns of growth and growing time. Performed in this way, companion planting is an extremely simple, trouble-free and cheap method of ensuring plant health.

In order to make such mixed cultivation possible, monoculture in beds is replaced by row-crop cultivation, in which the right plants will be properly spaced. As important as the superficial influence of one plant over another – say through their scents, which are perceptible by us – is the unseen but essential influence they bring to bear on each other down in the root region: through root exudations, through their differing nutrient requirements and through specific bacteria. What is more, they leave behind them a visible and an invisible legacy in the soil, ready for utilization by future generations. In row-crops changes take place both above and below ground (at the level of the micro-organisms). The companion-planted garden has to be considered not only in relation to what goes on in the space above the surface, but, more particularly, in relation to the demands made by the plants on the soil. To ensure that the most diverse root residues can be fed into the ground, and that decomposing vegetable matter and nutrients are present on and in the soil whatever the season, the garden must be well stocked with and covered in plant growth during the year.

The row widths must therefore be big enough to provide adequate surface compost the whole year through (see pages 35–38). Anything from the garden that is at all suitable is used as a covering and turned into compost; the garden keeps its contents to be recycled. Hence provision is made for the continuous nourishment of plant life, and manuring is managed with minimal expenditure of labour, using the rich natural humus from the garden. Even in the cold time of year there are some plants which are ready for cropping; others are still growing and there are seeds to be sown ready for spring. All things considered, spring seems to be the best place to start.

Spring and Early Summer
What, then, has to be done at the first signs of spring in order to set up a system of companion planting in the garden? As soon as the weather and the state of the

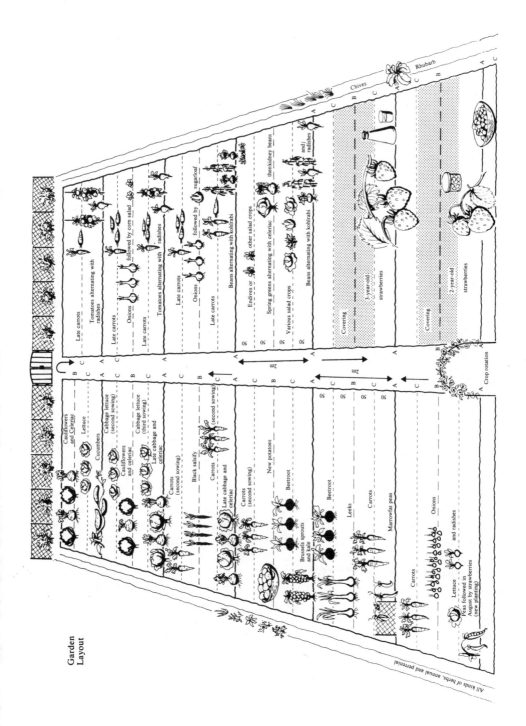

Garden Layout

soil allows (at least when the ground is dry enough to walk on), cultivation begins and continues without intermission for the rest of the year.

Sowing Spinach

Spinach is sown in spring in 50cm row widths over the whole garden area without leaving footpaths. As soon as the spinach seeds are up, hoeing is done between the rows with a flat hoe in order to deal with the first signs of weeds. This early sowing of spinach serves a number of purposes. In the first place, it marks obvious divisions right from the start, laying down clear dividing lines just as if they had been drawn with pen and ink on a sheet of paper. These rows divide the garden up for the whole year. The usual paths between individual beds are omitted. All the same, this type of cultivation leaves plenty of walking space. (See the section on companion planting in beds, page 29.) In the second place, since the whole garden is sown with spinach, the ground is bound together by a gradually developing network of roots which prevents the constituents of the soil from being washed away while at the same time preventing the land from becoming crusty. Ideally, the row width should be about 50cm, but 40cm is also satisfactory if the available space is limited.

In between the individual rows of spinach, which soon make their appearance, are the places for the main crops to be sown or planted during the year. The spinach, as it grows, provides the young plants with protection and shade; its foliage prevents the soil from drying out; it discourages certain pests and, finally, spinach provides material for sheet composting (on the soil surface) to be made *in situ*. Later on, it will be quite easy to cut and lay the spinach with a flat or a draw hoe.

Spinach roots are soft and no trace of them is left after a few days. The soil can be reworked, and the spinach, with its content of saponine and mucins and its soft mass of leaves, has a quick fertilizing effect. The decaying roots and the leaves which have been cut down provide early nourishment for soil organisms; these now become intensely active as the climate warms up. What was once a row of spinach now becomes an intermediate space, a footpath. It is in between these lines of spinach that the other vegetable varieties are arranged, as illustrated in the diagram.

The soil cover afforded by the spinach (and that means cover over all ground that is not sown or planted with other things) serves as shade, as a protection for soil life, as pathway protection, and as weather protection against hot sun and heavy rain; in addition, spinach increases the food supply of earthworms and of all other visible and invisible inhabitants of the soil. The whole garden is gradually overgrown and so the initial requirement of this type of cultivation is fulfilled.

At first, the beginner may dislike the absence of beds separated by paths, but he will soon see the advantage of having evenly nourished plants throughout the garden. The abandonment of beds and paths does away with the need for their upkeep during the year, and since there are no edges, there can be no edging plants; all plants therefore receive an equal amount of care and their roots can spread out in all directions to find what they need. With traditional paths, the earth is trodden down hard during the year and provides no sources of nutrition for adjacent plants. Also,they cannot be used for cultivation in the following year without a great deal of trouble. All this has to be taken into consideration, with special reference to the advantages of a thoroughgoing form of companion planting as advocated here.

The Cultivation Plan

Prior to deciding where the various crops will go, either by sketching a plan on paper or by marking the garden out with labels stuck in the ground between the rows of spinach, some consideration must be given to the best positions for the various plants, whether tall, low, flat or spreading (e.g. cucumbers). It is necessary to calculate when the plants will be ready.

The diagram on page 26 shows that the rows are given letters. Whatever is put in the A row can have had a preceding crop up to only a short time before the main crop goes in, but it needs its place from the middle of May to the end of the year. This A row is marked in red. The red colour also designates the main rows. They are two metres apart and are intended for such things as tomatoes, runner beans, cucumbers, late cabbage, broad beans, and perhaps potatoes and courgettes. It goes without saying that these rows, together with their partner crops, can be repeated as often as is desired (always two metres apart), according to the needs of the household or of customers (in the case of a market garden).

In between two A rows we have the B rows, marked green in the plan and on the garden labels. These B rows are intended for plants which are going to require this space either in the first half or in the second half of the growing year. Examples are: leeks, onions, black salsify cauliflower, celeriac, kidney beans, spring greens, beetroot, peas, parsnips. Each of these rows will yield at least two full crops.

Between the A rows and the B rows, at a distance of 50cm we have the C rows, which are given the colour blue. There are two C rows for every A and every B row. These are set with short-lived plants which a comparatively small, low growth. They persist for a short time only and then make way for other, similar plants. They like the light shade of the neighbouring plants which have already sprung up in rows A and B. Domestic needs are greatest for this type of vegetable and there is a succession of crops. After early varieties of one species, there follows a later variety of another species. (For example, spring carrots may be followed by a kind of late lettuce or other salad crops). These C rows will produce two and often three crops one after the other, consisting of such things as early, second-early and late carrots, bulbs raised from seed, all lettuce, cabbage lettuce of various sorts, endives, kohlrabi, fennel etc. When the main crop in the red A rows is cucumbers, the blue C rows to right and left are planted *once only*, because later on the cucumbers will need space for growth. The rather large number of so-called 'short-term' (or blue) rows is very important in this system: a great many mixed crops can be grown in them.

It should perhaps be stressed once more that there are many-sided, beneficial and well-balanced effects in that part of companion planting which is visible to the naked eye, but not in that part alone; further advantages arise from the encouragement given to the micro-organisms in the soil and it is through this that problems to do with the rotation of crops are also very largely solved.

The success or otherwise of a companion-planted garden depends on the row system. The labels must not be re-arranged during the year and there must always be double and successional sowing or planting in the same rows. The reason for this will become clear when we come to consider the nature of sheet composting (composting on the soil surface). In a garden of this kind, order is the first prerequisite for success; it makes the daily work so much easier.

The Beginning of the Gardening Year

Above:
It is still tulip time, and shrubs and bushes have come into leaf. The young spinach is clearly visible. In the intermediate spaces there are carrots, onions, lettuce and peas from early sowings to be seen. Mustard or field beans have been sown for pre-cropping in rows not yet set aside for the main crop.
Below left:
Companion planting of strawberries and leeks in the same row. Mustard fills the spaces between the rows.
Below right:
Later crops are added stage by stage. The early mustard is now cut down. The drills are prepared, sown, covered with earth and dressed with the residues of the mustard. The spinach will soon be ready to pull but meanwhile it separates and protects the other plants. The double label reads: kidney beans to be followed by a second crop (sugarloaf, chicory etc.).

Early Sowing

Once the spinach has been sown and after accurate partitioning and labelling of the ground, a start can be made on preparing for the early crops. These are carrots, onions, early lettuce, also onion seed for sets for planting. In the next few pages, some examples will be given to show in detail how a companion planting plan might look.

Carrots, say, are sown between the first and second rows of spinach. Then, between the second and third rows of spinach, either onions are sown or onion sets are put in or onion seed is sown to produce sets for planting. Carrots are again sown between the third and fourth rows. It is a well known fact, one which has been proved time and again, that onions and carrots give mutual protection to one another against carrot fly and onion fly respectively.

Between the fourth and fifth rows of spinach, the intermediate space of 50cm is left free. However, the red A label for tomatoes is put there. Because they make good neighbours for the tomatoes, more carrots are put in between the fifth and sixth spinach rows. In later carrot sowings, the same purpose is served with very good effect by sowing parsnips too. Parsnips are interchangeable with carrots as a companion plant. What is more, they have a remarkably deep growth (up to 80cm long and completely undamaged roots are no exception). The parsnip is also fairly resistant to pests.

Above left:
Work begins in the vegetable patch. Quick-germinating spinach is sown in 50cm row widths (or 40cm widths in smaller gardens). The spinach has a double function at this stage: it acts as an early source of fresh food and as protection and shade for the main crops, which will follow later. The twine, which is still in place, marks the rows of spinach. Between the rows, seed for the earliest outdoor plants has been sown. See plan (page 13).

Below left:
The spinach has grown. Early carrots, onions, lettuce, radishes and early peas (but as yet no marrowfat peas) have appeared. Mustard seed is broadcast in all rows not yet ready for the principal crops. The main values of this are in the way the soil is broken up by the roots, the shade afforded to the soil preserving its humidity, and the disinfectant action of the mustard oil.

Above right:
The mustard has come up and three rows of young strawberry plants are plainly visible in the background. They were planted in the previous year in between the leeks, after the peas had been harvested.

Below right:
The first weeds can be removed with a hoe after the spinach and other early crops have appeared.

Alternatively, the space between the first and second rows of spinach can be left free for the later planting of celeriac and cauliflowers. The cauliflowers will help to ward off celery rust on the one hand and the celeriac will stop infestations of caterpillars (cabbage white). This would be a B row (green).

Between the second and third rows of spinach comes the first sowing of cabbage lettuce or of some 'cut and come again' variety of lettuce (open-leaf), always mixed with radishes of the small or large early variety. The lettuce will give good protection to the radishes against flea beetle. The row between the third and fourth rows of spinach remains free for cucumbers, and so a red label for an A row is stuck in the ground. It is a good idea to put cutting lettuce in this empty A row as a first crop, in a strip several centimetres wide, with radish sown amongst it (once more for protection).

Now, should the gardener decide to sow some land cress instead of lettuce as a preliminary crop, this would not be advisable (the reason is given later in the section dealing with the cultivation of medicinal and culinary herbs). Lettuce and early radishes would come between the fourth and fifth rows of spinach. Both rows of salad plants are ready by the time the cucumbers need the space, which is earmarked by the red label between the third and fourth rows of spinach. The space between the fifth and sixth rows of spinach remains free for celeriac, cauliflowers or spring greens. Cabbage white butterflies are deterred from laying their eggs on brassicas when celeriac is growing in the immediate vicinity. This next row would be a 'green' or B row. In planting more than one type of thing at the same time, the spring greens soon vacate their place, whereas the celeriac goes on to develop its roots in the place left to it.

If, for some reason or other, no marker rows of spinach have been sown (the weather, say, or some personal problem having prevented it), there is naturally nothing to stop companion planting being carried out as described. The *imaginary* rows of spinach are left clear until some other covering material is available. Spinach is not absolutely essential to the correct formation of a mixed culture, but the fertility of the soil is certainly improved when spinach seed is sown.

All these examples show the idea behind companion planting, which is to place the right plants in the right environment as regards local requirements, timing, and vacation of the space occupied so that other plants can be put in. In the first place, care must be taken to achieve the correct combination, so that every plant can protect the plant next to it, and light and shade are so distributed that they fall where the plants need them.

Another good mixture deserving mention is runner beans with spring greens of all sorts. A (red) A row is taken for the runner beans, early cabbages are put in on either side of them one metre away in the B rows, while 50cm away in the blue rows, go cabbage lettuce, radishes, kohlrabi (see the section about the advantages of direct sowing on page 20). After the C row salad plants have been cropped, these rows are left free to leave room for picking the beans. As soon as the spring greens have been gathered, there is plenty of space for sowing winter radishes and endives.

A further very good example of mixed planting is to have tomatoes in the A rows two metres apart, then onion seed or sets in rows one metre to the left and right (to produce onion bulbs for the coming year), and 50cm away (in the blue C rows) early, second-early and late carrots or turnip-rooted parsley or – and this is a really inspired choice – parsnips.

Here is one more example. Place peas in the A rows: early peas or perhaps the taller-growing and later marrowfat peas (although marrowfat peas are sensitive to frost and must not be sown too early!). One metre away in the (green) B rows, plant a mixed crop of cabbages or cauliflowers and celeriac, and 50cm away in the blue C rows sow beetroot and lettuce, to be followed later by kohlrabi sown direct and then thinned.

The celeriac, which has been mentioned several times already, can be made to produce roots to meet the winter's needs, when planted as a mixed crop in the rows of cauliflowers or spring greens; when the early greens are picked the celeriac then has more room to grow.

Incompatibility

The companion crops mentioned so far are based on observations made over many years and they have proved their worth. Better growth was marked when the correct combination of plants was used; on the other hand, with the wrong combination, growth can actually be hindered, so wrong combinations are to be avoided at all costs. There are several unfavourable combinations which need to be remembered:

Beans and onions
Cabbages and onions
Red cabbages and tomatoes
Parsley and cabbage lettuce
Beetroots and tomatoes
Potatoes and onions

It is not good to put in spinach as a preliminary crop before beetroot, mangolds, or orach ('fat hen').

If these few negative combinations are avoided, not many mistakes will be made.

Celeriac and Tomatoes as Protective Plants
Celeriac is used to ward caterpillars off all kinds of brassicas. Celeriac plants will not always grow into large roots when put in with late varieties of cabbage, and we do not expect them to do so, but use them as a form of protection and for supplying green leaves for the kitchen during the winter. In this way, they act as a sure defence against the cabbage white butterfly. Celery, which is planted for the sake of the sticks, is left to grow undisturbed and its leaves are not picked.

The tomato, too, is an outstanding protective plant! Therefore, plants at risk can be put between the tomatoes in the rows (e.g. various types of cabbage), just as celeriac is set between infestation-prone cabbage. Anyone who has seen how a plant of a certain species can afford protection against insect and fungus pests and diseases of certain other plants, will hardly fail to take advantage of such an easy method of pest control in future. What is more, these easy methods are not only cost-free, but are non-polluting to the environment!

This type of defence works firstly through the right choice of protective plant and secondly on account of the considerable distances maintained between rows of the same plant, impeding the spread of infestations or fungal infections. The success obtained in a companion-planted garden is often quite amazing. For a long time, all this was no more than a matter of experience, but now it has been given scientific backing, according to a report in the American magazine *Organic Gardening* (Rodale Press, Emmaus, Pa., U.S.A.). It is claimed that every plant possesses its own unique active substances and scents (often perceptible to us) which it sheds into its environment. An insect orientates itself to these scents as they are wafted through the air, and seeks out its own special plants on which it feeds or lays its eggs. For our purposes it is a pest. Now, if there are other plants nearby producing completely different scents and secretions, the insect becomes confused. It is deterred by the resulting combination of perfumes and moves further afield. What goes on at root level, undetected by us, is also important and even decisive in the reciprocal effect of each plant on its neighbours.

The Advantages of Direct Sowing
When examples of companion crops were given, 'sowing' was repeatedly mentioned. Perhaps this needs further explanation. One of the advantages of planting in rows is that as one cropping time succeeds another, the various rows become available for fresh sowing and planting. It is then easy to sow direct varieties of vegetable which would formerly have been planted out, for instance lettuces, cucumbers, kohlrabi and so on. Mixed cropping within the rows is always possible here (this will be dealt with in detail in Chapter 4).

Lettuce is especially suitable for direct sowing. A row of radishes will do well when this direct sowing is carried out, because the lettuce wards off the flea-beetle. What is more, properly thinned, direct sown lettuce will grow well without showing the gaps which can be caused when planting out is done carelessly (or the plants are damaged by improper watering). The plants grow without check and are not devoured by snails or undermined by earthworms or plagued by any similar problems.

With direct sowing, whenever this is possible, it will always be found that what is sown will have an advantage over what is planted out *at the same time.* Neither pests nor diseases trouble the sown plants, and all the problems which beset lettuce (such as mildew, greenfly etc.) do not arise when the seed is sown straight into the ground together with the seeds of other suitable vegetables as described later.

Avoiding Crop Rotation Problems

The companion planter hardly needs to give much thought to whether or not he is using the right method of crop rotation. If he has done his planting as recommended and has observed the proper spacing between the long-term, middle-term and short-term rows, crop rotation will look after itself.

Repeated cultivation of the rows within the same gardening year has already given good crop rotation results. The practical gardener would also be well advised to label the rows with the names of the varieties to be put in during the whole year in sequence, using for this purpose labels coloured as suggested (see illustrations) and putting them in place at the beginning of the year when the land is first divided up and sown. The labels should be left in position right through the year. The gardener will experience no difficulty with crop rotation if he changes his crops two or three times in the same row and if, in the following year, he displaces the spinach rows and the vegetable rows half a measure sideways – i.e. about 25cm away from where they were before. In this way, the next year's spinach occupies this year's vegetable row. Thus the vegetable crops are planted or sown in the surface compost from the previous year. In practice, therefore, it is extremely unlikely that the same or a closely related plant will occupy the same place again. In case there has been no preliminary sowing of spinach, the vegetable row is put in where the surface compost was. The old division between 'heavy feeders' and 'weak feeders' can be forgotten.

As will be explained more fully in the section on sheet composting, the companion-planted garden is quite uniformly fertilized so that the gardener does not have to be unduly concerned about manuring and crop rotation, and all his crops show healthy and even growth. He has found out that so many things are a lot simpler in this companion planting system.

Late Summer, Autumn and Winter

Towards the end of the gardening year, as autumn approaches, a garden has been established according to the basic ideas of companion planting as already explained. The garden is not only time-saving to work but in fine condition for next year's crops. As we can see from the plan on page 26 and the illustrations, such a garden is not divided up into beds but into exactly spaced rows which do not vary in the course of the year. Thus the main rows (the red, A rows) are laid out at two metre intervals. These rows have a brief first crop that is gathered by the end of May, which then makes way for the principal crop. Examples of this type of crop are tomatoes, cucumbers and late brassicas of all sorts. The middle (green or B rows) are laid down between the A rows at distances of one metre. These are used for vegetables which may be cropped early in the year.

Harvesting the Second Crops

The B rows now bear the second crops which will be gathered in autumn: fennel, Chinese cabbage, parsnips, lettuce (the later varieties) endives, chicory, dill. These crops were preceded by such quick-growing crops as cutting lettuce, cress and mustard. In some cases they have a somewhat later planting time, i.e. leeks, celeriac, later cauliflower and beetroot (which can be harvested a little earlier too).

Finally, there is a partial crop from the so-called short-term rows, in other words from the C rows situated between the main and the middle rows at a distance of 50cm. These produce all the early varieties of lettuce, radishes, various sorts of carrot, kohlrabi and kidney beans etc.First crops of these vegetables have long since been gathered in and the rows have yielded two or even three crops. Now they are producing late carrots, different sorts of lettuces (always with radishes), freshly sown herbs such as dill, plus kohlrabi and spinach for autumn use. So, even in autumn, the companion-planted garden is still producing a full range of fresh vegetables.

As the individual rows are harvested, the gardener will consider whether or not it would be worth while to sow for yet another crop. There is bound to come a time when, even in the most favourable climates, what comes up will not be any good and so the rows will start dropping out of use.

An End to Digging!

It must be remembered that a garden should be green all through the year. Therefore, when a row has been harvested, it should not be left bare and brown, and much less should the soil be turned over. This would only serve to bury the active soil under a layer of inactive soil! Therefore when a row is no longer required, it should simply be prodded with a garden fork; the fork handle is moved about a bit to disturb the soil without turning it, and then the fork is pulled out each time. This work of loosening the soil with a fork can be performed even by those who are elderly or frail. There is no heavy digging to do.

Sowing Mustard

At this time of year, when even the short-term vegetables are over, some long-term seeds can still begin to germinate and even a slight growth is to be expected. In this now *ventilated* soil, mustard seed is broadcast. Some of it falls into the airholes made with the fork and the remainder needs only to be lightly raked over. The mustard germinates in a few days to give a thick green cover.

In this way, the land is cared for in the best possible manner: it is overgrown with green to hold the weeds down, the roots keep the soil broken up and the soil is shaded to prevent it from drying out. Also, since the mustard will not flower, which can hardly be expected at this time of year, it will consume less water than would run off bare topsoil. Mustard creates a 'miniature woodland' with a moist and shady floor.

In comparison with other green manuring plants, all of which have their value, mustard has one or two other advantages for the garden. None other is so simple to sow or so easy to manage as the soft mustard, which is nipped by the frost at $-7°C$. The easy management is especially important in companion-planted gardens which only require light tools. What is more, mustard leaves behind no thick stalks for the spring if care is taken to stop it flowering. The light layer of vegetable matter lying on the frozen ground will fall to powder at the gentlest motion of the rake. No other preparation is needed for sowing; everything has already been done without any fuss and bother in the autumn.

This process continues: whenever a row is released from the annual round of sowing because it is too late for another crop, the soil is ventilated and sown with mustard – as long as there is a chance that the seed will still germinate. Even when the seedlings are no more than a few centimetres high, the roots go much deeper and provide a valuable root residue.

A note for housewives: These small mustard plants, growing so late in the year are a very welcome supplement to the diet in the form of salads and pot herbs; they are mellower than cress and have less bite. What is more, they make a valuable contribution to health and are especially useful at this time of year when the garden's vitamin producers are in gradual recession.

Finally, the last few rows are left in readiness for the winter. They can no longer be inter-sown with green manuring crops, since these would not be able to survive, not even quick-germinating mustard. These last rows will be of celeriac, late cabbage and possibly beetroot or carrots for the winter store. The soil in these rows has already been prepared for the spring sowing, when the fork lifting the autumn crops ventilated the soil; however, a little extra attention may now be in order to ensure that enough air is worked into the soil. The rows are now neatly and evenly covered with the leaves which have been twisted off and discarded; thus each row has its own leafy cover.

So now at the beginning of winter there are several green rows of variously advanced mustard, there are rows hidden under leaves and there are rows of plants growing on for winter (leeks, kale, Brussels sprouts, parsley).

By spring, the surface mulch (sheet compost) will have rotted down unless the winter has been very snowy with a blanket of snow from November to February. The frozen green mustard forms a light protective veil over the ground and even the vegetable rows are covered with their own leaves to give a well frozen cover of rotted matter. As far as the garden as a whole is concerned, all that is necessary is to rake over the surface. A small but useful quantity of material for the compost heap is provided by the rakings.

At this point, gardeners may be asking what happens in winter to the 50cm wide intermediate spaces made up with surface compost. These rows also serve as paths; spinach grows in them in spring and the composition of their covering is most varied. Like any other compost, the mulch composting on the surface has been built up and processed layer by layer as rottable substances have become available. All the material gathered has already rotted by autumn, and the soil is nice and loose with a good stock of earthworms. If necessary these strips will also be ventilated with the garden fork. In this way, the otherwise heavy and difficult autumn labour will be avoided, the ground will be prepared for the coming year and crop rotation will cease to be a headache.

Sowing in Frosty Soil for an Early Spring Crop
In regions with hard soil, it is often possible to walk about the garden very early in spring, so an attempt should be made to introduce seed in the soil at a time when the frost is already making an impression (see illustration facing page 33) i.e. in December at the earliest. During this season, seeds can no longer germinate and this suits the gardener's purposes at this time; at most, the seed swells ready for spring when the weather is sufficiently warm, at which time it will really start to grow.

For this seed the soil should be lightly frozen and dry. The ground is covered with soil, not with peat or turf as this retains the cold to a high degree, retards germination and can place the success of the whole project in jeopardy. Furthermore, no compost of any sort is used for a covering, but the soil that has been developed *in situ* is ideal. The rows provided for the early sowing of lettuce and carrots are sowed with an *early variety* from December onwards. This is quite important because winter cabbage lettuce is not sown just on account of the fact that it is winter, but the earliest variety of outdoor lettuce and very early carrots are sown. This sowing is carried out before the ground is ready for walking on in spring. The seeds have a demonstrable three weeks start in germination – or thereabouts. Therefore, there is no need to worry over getting on with the cultivation of the vegetable plot in spring, since the most important seeds are already in the ground.

The varieties of vegetable chosen for sowing in frosty soil are those which will not be sensitive to relatively low temperatures after the young plants have started to sprout. Plants which have proved their worth in cold conditions are the earliest varieties of lettuce, the earliest varieties of carrot, also spinach, leeks, black salsify, turnip-rooted parsley and kohlrabi, which tend not to sprout when the temperatures are low. When these conditions are respected, even spring greens can be produced. It goes without saying that parsley and onions can be sown in winter. In many years the Stuttgart Giant variety has done well.

Cropping Times

Companion planting, using the recommended spacing to keep infections at bay, offers further advantages in addition to plant health. For example, there is always *one* row (especially with the short-term crops) which is ready for picking at regular intervals to leave room for fresh sowings. This type of garden is one of continual cropping and sowing, and since the basic rows are always ready, many crops can be sown direct and can grow and mature where they are – without any need for planting out.

Another advantage is that, with sowing in rows in a companion-planted garden, the housewife can keep pace with the rate at which her produce becomes ready. Here there are no large beds but only rows yielding their produce when wanted. Thus the garden is not stocked with beds half full of unpicked lettuce or cauliflower, which will hold up re-use of the land.

Whatever the vegetable, it should be picked when the climax of growth is reached but not passed. This requirement too is easily satisfied. The opportunity given by this gardening method for all produce to be picked at the right time, means that it comes to the table in peak condition.

Growing Onions

Onions are not only useful but indispensable in nutrition. Onion plants, in all their varieties, are also indispensable in the garden, as we have seen on page 17. A good place for planting onions of all sorts, not so far considered, is in the strawberry beds or rows. The photograph opposite page 16 with the onion-like leeks in rows of freshly planted strawberries shows that there are no problems

Plants which Make Good Neighbours

Beans/Brassicas	Lettuce/Kidney beans
Brassicas/Beetroot	Lettuce/Beetroot
Tomatoes/Parsley	Lettuce/Mangolds
Tomatoes/Onions	Peas/Brassicas
Tomatoes/Brassicas	Peas/Celery
Tomatoes/Celeriac	Celery/All types of greens, especially
Tomatoes/Kidney beans	when mixed in the rows
Carrots/Onions	Cucumbers/Brassicas
Parsnips/Onions	Potatoes/All types of brassicas
Lettuce/Radish	(late varieties)
Lettuce/Beans	Potatoes/Peas
Lettuce/Cucumbers	Potatoes/Broad beans

Types of Vegetable, divided according to
main rows (A), middle rows (B) and short-term rows (C)

A rows
RED, spaced at 2 metres, from May to the end of the vegetation period, for tall or bushy plants. Pre-sown with mustard or broad beans in early spring.
Tomatoes, runner beans, cucumbers, late cabbage, broad beans, potatoes, courgettes, early peas and marrowfat peas.

B rows
GREEN, spaced at 2 metres, two full crops in the first and second halves of the growing year.
Leeks (sown rows), onions, black salsify, cauliflower, celery, kidney beans, spring greens, beetroot, parsnips, mangolds, onion sets raised from seed.

C rows
BLUE, spaced at 1 metre, plants with a short growing time and low growth.
Early carrots, lettuce, late carrots, onion sets raised from seed, cabbage lettuce and endives, kohlrabi, fennel, parsnips and leeks (sown rows).

over space and light requirements. The leeks are tall and compact, whereas the strawberries need to spread over the ground. They live together in a sort of symbiosis with striking benefit. It is quite obvious that the strawberries are not attacked by nematodes when plants of the onion family are in the vicinity. The strawberries are bushy and have a good display of flowers and fruit. They are protected from fungi to the extent that they occupy an exposed situation. As soon as strawberries are sheltered from air movement by such things as hedges and fences they are liable to fungal attack. Leeks are easy to plant: the young plants are trimmed and placed in liquid comfrey manure, a hole is then made with a dibber and the plants are inserted and watered. In the course of time the ground will be well washed in by the rain.

The result of this mode of cultivation may be seen opposite page 16: strawberries growing with leeks, which are ready to harvest in spring. The leeks should be dug up with a small implement which will cut them just above root level. The root remains in the soil next to the strawberry roots and can rot there. Strawberry rows that are left for several years, are cleared and thinned in autumn to make room for leeks or onions again. The illustration shows strawberries and leeks; strawberries and onions would have been equally possible. Onions set between strawberry plants always provide good crops.

As already mentioned, a ready supply of plants is a decisive factor in the cultivation of leeks and onions. Leeks are grown in their own seed rows from spring onwards, and plants can be taken from them right through to autumn as required. Since onions (as sets for planting) can be planted not only in spring as is usually done, but also in autumn, onion seed should also be sown in spring to produce sets for autumn planting. The crop of bulbs for planting is divided into two parts: one part is stored for spring planting and the other part is put in in early autumn in much the same way as is done in spring. The Stuttgart Giant variety and the spring variety, Express, are good for autumn production. The names of the varieties are given in this instance, because they have proved their worth in my locality and I know little about other varieties. With autumn planting, we get very early onions in spring and these, with their fresh green stalks, are packed with vitamins and other healthful factors. This early crop of two varieties becomes available before the old winter stored crop is used up and before the normal summer crop of onions is ready.

The question is often asked, why onions so easily run to seed. The reason can be a wrong choice of variety. Usually however, as long experience has shown, the bulbs are too big when planted. Bulbs for planting should be no bigger than a hazelnut. It is better to take out those that are too large and send them to the kitchen. If this advice is followed, it is entirely possible to have even growth within the rows.

A quality comparison between home-grown onion sets and those purchased from some unknown source, invariably favours the home-grown variety, especially as far as keeping is concerned. Naturally, fresh manure is to be avoided for this crop.

In this way, the back garden will supply all the onions required – and the companion-planted rows will supply many types of salad crops right through the year.

Growing Tomatoes

Many gardeners complain at the unhealthy state of their tomatoes. They suffer from leaf mosaic disease or the leaves drop off, the fruit are blighted and rotten. The damage is worst when the monoculture system of planting is used, especially when the tomatoes are put in too close together for any reason and the nutrient-hungry plants are not properly manured. In companion-planted gardens the rows of tomatoes are separated by some two metres. If tomatoes are much in demand, more mixed rows can be put in. Up to the time of planting with tomatoes, the rows are pre-planted with mustard or field beans and fertilized with a liquid manure made from stinging-nettles (*Urtica dioica*). Hardly any plant disease can take hold thanks to this pre-planting and advance manuring, and to the wide spacing of the rows and the separation of similar plants by plants of a different species. The air can move freely between the rows and the atmosphere around the tomatoes does not become so stale that disease is encouraged. Since tomatoes have proved their worth as defence plants against animal pests, other plants in need of such protection should be placed between them in the rows, e.g. kohlrabi or cauliflower and any other members of the cabbage family which do not grow too big. These other plants must be removed at the right time to make room for the mature growth of the tomatoes.

The quality of the young tomato plants is important: they ought to be dark green, fairly compact, firm and strong and already be showing signs of blossom. There is no certainty that bought plants will meet these requirements. However, it is not always possible to raise the tomatoes oneself. If possible, bought plants will be potted on again, especially if they have been boxed in peat. Tomatoes should not be planted out before 20 May to make sure they will not be harmed by late frosts, and they must be planted deep in the ground, so that the young flowers are no more than a hand's breadth above the level of the soil. They should be 'watered' with diluted liquid nettle fertilizer.

Plants which have grown too tall may also be used if they are set sloping in the ground and then covered to within a hand's breadth of the young flowers. The upper part will right itself in a few days. After the tomatoes have been put in, the rows are also sown with mustard and with marigolds (*Calendula officinalis*). Both species will later serve as a sort of mulch, for tomatoes should always stand in covered soil. When more covering material becomes available later on, especially in the form of medicinal herbs, the rows can be kept covered over their whole width right through summer.

Since tomatoes, like all other plants, need their leaves to help them produce well, it is absurd to pluck their leaves to let the sun ripen their fruit. The tomato side-shoots are nipped off from the axils of the leaves, but plenty of leaves must be left to manufacture food for the plants. Therefore, the lowest three to five side shoots can be left until they start to flower; the side shoots are then pruned above the first leaf.

The foliage must be left intact and pruning is continually carried out on the main stem which comes in the leaf axil. The plant is tied up as is the custom. In this way, not only are the first flowers and fruit hanging from the lower portion of the main stem, but also four or five lower side shoots (not yet stopped) will have started to come into flower as well. Hence the tomatoes are left with as many leaves as will be required to nourish them. Early in the season, you will be able to count a great number of fruit, all coming along nicely. This is a case in point where mixed cropping makes gardening so much easier.

Companion Planting in Beds

In what has been said so far, we have taken for granted the possession of free space which can be cultivated in spring just as we like, so that we can discard the old methods and get on with the new. However, there are some garden owners who are not prepared to abandon their flower beds, and there are gardens in which the beds are set in concrete surrounds or perhaps between crazy pavements. The question is, is it still possible to practise companion planting in such circumstances? One of the illustrations in this book, taken like all the others in our own garden, shows a corner with beds surrounded by paths laid with slabs. The beds were meant for growing roses throughout the year. Until the roses were planted, we endeavoured to work out what the difference was between companion planting in beds with fixed edges and an open plot where one can make a start in spring wherever desired. Various results have been obtained in three years of tests.

Anyone who intends to practise mixed cultivation in clearly defined beds must take special care, firstly that the correct plant communities are put in and secondly that the plants being grown along the edges of the beds do not have a spreading network of roots but occupy only a small amount of room, e.g. leeks, onions or carrots. The border is also a good place for parsley or many other low herbs. However, plants with big root systems which are supposed to spread all around are not suitable for borders. For example, celeriac should not stand near concrete slabs or at the edge of a path, as in this position it is liable to suffer from

Layout Examples for a Companion-planted Vegetable Garden

The types of vegetable are chosen and placed in relation to one another so that they are spaced to best advantage for protection against pests and disease and according to the individual requirements of each species. The combinations given below are carefully balanced. They can be repeated or alternated but must not be divided as far as the block units are concerned. (See page 26 and the diagram on page 66).

Example 1
C Carrots
B Onions
C Carrots
A reserved for tomatoes,
    pre-sown mustard or
    field beans
C Parsnips

Example 2
B Celery and cauliflower
    or other early greens
C Lettuce with radish
A reserved for cucumbers,
    pre-sown mustard or
    field beans
C Lettuce with radish
B Celery and cauliflower
    or other early greens
C Carrots, lettuce (several sowings)

Example 3
A Early peas followed by
    corn salad, pre-sown field
    beans or mustard
C Beetroot, lettuce
B Red cabbage with celeriac
C Beetroot, lettuce
A Marrowfat peas or late cabbage
C Beetroot, lettuce
B Cauliflower with celeriac
C Early lettuce

Example 4
A Runner beans
C Cabbage lettuce, radish
B Early cabbage or mangold
C Cabbage lettuce, other salads,
    including endives, kohlrabi

Example 5
A Tomatoes, broad beans
C Carrots, turnip-rooted parsley
B Young onions (for winter)
C Parsnips
A Courgettes
C Carrots, parsnips
B Onions grown from seed

Example 6
A Early potatoes, followed by
    corn salad (pre-sown field beans)
C Early lettuce, spinach
B reserved for Brussels sprouts
    and other brassicas for autumn
    and winter use, after the
    potatoes have been earthed up
C Endives (bedded out from rows
    of seedlings)

rust, especially when the heat of the sun warms up the slabs in summer.

Those who cannot bring themselves to do without garden paths can, without altering the companion planting system or our way of treating the soil, lay a plank gangway over the surface compost between every few rows. As soon as enough top covering material is available, the planks will become unnecessary. An adequate provision of covering material is very important, because the soil between the plants needs to be covered in cases where beds are retained. The correct covering materials will prevent the soil drying out and will also tend to add to its water content by collecting dew.

When using beds, less soil is available for plant roots, but this disadvantage can be offset by building up a fine, nutrient-rich soil. Earthworm compost, for example (see pages 44–45), may be spread wherever there is room, and fresh leaves and half-made compost can also be applied to make good the deficiencies so often found in beds.

A good example of companion planting in flower beds set between flagstones is to have roses as the main plant in the middle rows underplanted with all sorts of narcissi (but not tulips as these are attractive to mice). The beds can be edged with sage for its fragrance and because it attracts bees but discourages pests. Another example would be old-fashioned roses, underplanted with bugle (*Ajuga reptans*), with the addition of day lilies (*Hemerocallis*), which do best in corners where they have more room to grow. Equally splendid perennials for our purposes are Madonna lilies (*Lilium candidum*) and dittany (*Dictamnus albus*). As before, the edging should be done with perennial herbs. Sage has already been mentioned, and lavender, hyssop and thyme are also suitable for adorning our borders and improving our health.

Where a garden has already been laid out in beds which the owner does not wish to disturb, it is still possible to carry out companion planting of flowers or vegetables which will give each other mutual support. However, when we have a free choice, we can go in for the much more advantageous companion planting in open ground and practise the trouble-free rotation of crops.

2.
Soil Cover, Composting and Watering

Since the experienced, organically-minded gardener knows that thriving, healthy plants with a good yield depend on the life of the soil, and this in turn partly depends on its humus content, he or she will strive to improve the soil by keeping it continually covered with growing plants. Soil that is broken up by roots and shaded by leaves produces vigorous plants in good time, and as these grow and then die, the organisms in the soil work to liberate all kinds of active substances from the dead vegetation. The channels excavated by roots allow the passage of air and water, both necessary for the transportation and exchange of nutrients and, indeed, for the maintenance of life.

The gardener who adopts this way of working knows also that the land must not be left bare and unprotected, but must be provided with protective cover and shade. This covering provides food for the population of earthworms that is so essential to good gardening. A constant cover of vegetation and surface compost are the only measures which can bring about a noticeable and enduring improvement in the soil.

Early Summer
The herbs sown with the main crops are clearly visible: dill and marigolds with the carrots, and borage and celery with the cabbages. The tomatoes have been undersown with short-term mustard. The marigolds will soon be removed from where they are growing among the carrots to be spread under the tomatoes as a surface mulch is vitally important for their healthy and trouble-free growth. The spinach has already been chopped from all the intermediate rows, which are now covered with a litter of grass cuttings and wild flowers. At present the ground is covered with chopped organic material, but chopped perennials and even wood chips may be added later, (see page 42).

Preparatory Sowing

Rows of spinach and first early sowings cover only part of the ground, but there is nothing to prevent the gardener from covering the rest of the space with vegetation. In the empty gaps between the rows of spinach, where no early crops are yet growing – whether lettuce, radishes or carrots – because they are not yet needed, some preliminary sowings can be made.

Mustard

Quick-germinating mustard is sown fairly thickly and in a few days it provides a neat thick green cover. Mustard fulfils all requirements for a plant that will help to keep the soil in good condition. Preparatory sowings should be made early as this allows time for the soil to be well broken up by roots; the ground retains its moisture, and the mustard tends to ward off snails and other pests. Mustard is easy to remove before sowing or planting other crops. These are advantages which should not be ignored. It is especially important at this time of year, when starting companion planting, that the various kinds of vegetable put in for different purposes should help one another and not get in one another's way. No square foot of earth need be left fallow as long as planting is carried out in an orderly and systematic manner. I shall return to the value of mustard later on when dealing with herbs.

In the meantime, the spinach continues to grow. Mustard sown on those rows

Autumn Preparations for the Spring

Prod holes in the ground but do not dig. Cover with greenery as far as possible.
Top left:
In late autumn, the following remain for harvesting in winter: leeks, red cabbage, endives, sugar loaf and parsley.
All the harvested rows are well prodded with a fork without turning the soil. The outside leaves of the previously picked plants can be spread on top of the forked soil.
Centre left and top right:
Mustard is broadcast on the ventilated, undulating land that has not been raked up. This can be repeated over and over again right up to and into October.
Centre right:
Mustard freezes at –19.5 °F (–7°C). It forms a light carpet in winter which allows the air to penetrate the ground. In spring the remnants crumble under the rake and the plot can be tilled early on, in good time, without any other working of the soil.
Below left and below right:
The left-hand photograph shows the ground properly prepared: although lightly frozen, it must still be capable of being drilled. The seeds must be covered with the garden soil itself, not with peat or compost! Tread it down firmly.
All early produce is sown, such as cabbage lettuce (early varieties, including Attraction), early carrots, kohlrabi that will not run to seed, early peas.

which are not yet needed, will usually give way when the main crops are sown or planted. For general purposes, therefore, the mustard should not be allowed to grow more than hand-high. It is no more than a preliminary plant, sown to prepare the ground and to keep it loose, moist and free from weeds. Any type of vegetable may be put in after it, without any worries over crop rotation. Whether planted before or between other crops, mustard always has a regenerating effect and, when the time comes to replace it, it may be chopped down and left to lie where it is. It will not interfere with subsequent drilling or digging and the soil in which it has been grown will give a good start to any other young plants and enable their root systems to spread out quickly and evenly.

In this connection, it is worth dealing with a question that is constantly being raised. In all gardens there are several kinds of cabbages plus radishes and other cruciferous plants; some garden flowers also belong to the *Cruciferae*. But many gardens in this country are infected with that bane of the crucifers, club root. Hence it may seem senseless to increase the stock of cruciferous plants by deliberately sowing mustard. What, then, have we learnt from long experience that encourages us to persist in sowing it?

Even though it has been established in practice that mustard – in spite of being a crucifer – can not be held responsible for damage to other cruciferous plants (e.g. for club root in cabbages), a further word of explanation is due to the reader. Experience has shown that it is always the release of hormones and other active substances which is good (or on occasion, bad) for the environment; so it is not the 'family' to which a plant has been assigned that matters, but the nature of the chemicals it contains. Classification of plants under the *Cruciferae* or some other family, is a device for helping us in the rapid naming of species (Linnaeus). The botanical dictionary clearly states that it is no more than an aid to identification. Those *Cruciferae* with which we are concerned are so varied in the chemical composition of their natural products that the fact that we call them cruciferae does not enable us to say if their effects will be positive or negative. For instance, in this family we have food or culinary plants (such as the familiar cabbage, radish and rape), medicinal plants (such as scurvy grass, once eaten by seafarers to prevent scurvy) and many weeds or rather healing herbs, not to mention garden flowers, such as wall-flowers, especially those of the early blossoming kind, and dye plants such as the rose of Jericho. This plant would scarcely be recognized as a member of the *Cruciferae*, neither is it thought of as a menace to cabbages; the same is true of many other flowers and therefore any worries over mustard are unfounded.

Another problem is often discussed in connection with mustard. Gardens generally are not plagued with nematodes plain and simple, but these pests come in many shapes and forms. Therefore, no single plant exists that will inhibit *all* nematodes, and the gardener has to know how to recognize the different types of nematode and which individual plants are effective against them.

The advantages of sowing mustard are that it disinfects and regenerates the soil, it stimulates the life of the soil and curbs nematodes, especially potato root eelworm, which is why it is so useful to sow the seed broadcast. It gives the feared nematodes very little chance in the garden. Its effect on all plant life, including the crucifers, is not negative but positive.

Field Beans
Another suitable plant for early sowing as a green manure crop would be one belonging to the *Leguminosae*; the field bean (*Vicia faba minor*) is a fine example. This preparatory crop has proved itself to be very beneficial to all vegetables which, coming later in the year, need a good supply of nourishment and are helped by a predecessor which ensures this nourishment, especially when it contains liberal amounts of the element nitrogen.

The field bean is a nitrogen-storing plant with roots that strike fairly deep and a rich stock of nitrogen bacteria, which release nitrogen into the soil for the benefit of all neighbouring plants or following crops. To put in field beans is to provide a natural nitrate fertilizer and no difficulty is involved in this preliminary sowing. Field beans can be sown very early in the year, and they are not damaged by spring frosts. They are deep-rooted and if they are allowed to grow to 30 to 40cm high and are then chopped down, they are still soft and rot quickly.

When the time has come for putting in the later vegetables such as late cabbage and especially fruit-bearing plants like tomatoes and cucumbers, the preliminary rows of beans are cut down. The residue is left lying where it is, and the results of this prior sowing of beans or fruit-bearing crops and also on various types of cabbage will be excellent if my experience is anything to go by. The performance of the plants in regard to yield, weight and (above all) health has been well above average.

The gardener will be happy to have at his or her disposal a wide range of vegetables, thanks to the favourable soil conditions created by leguminous plants. The meagre numbers of peas and beans traditionally grown has not been sufficient in the past to guarantee a full quota of nitrogen.

Other Preparatory Sowings
It goes without saying that other preparatory crops are possible, such as garden cress and many medicinal herbs and flowers. However, most of these suffer from the disadvantage that they vacate the place required for the main crops

rather too late. Cress grows just as quickly as mustard, but it is a very aggressive herb! As a preparatory crop it is suitable *only for quite stable following crops*, which, in practice, means tomatoes. If cress is sown before cucumbers, the cucumbers will die very shortly, and the same applies to other delicate crops.

It has been observed that many types of plants 'do not follow themselves well' and this is especially true of cress. When it is sown in spring, it should never be sown a second time in the same container or the same row – it is aggressive against itself. On the other hand, an example of a neutral and quick-growing plant is phacelia (*Phacelia tanacetifolia*),* which makes a dense but easily removed protective cover for the soil when used as a preparatory crop.

Phacelia is an old half-forgotten plant which is particularly valuable in the garden. The fine seed can be sown very early and at other times during the year thereafter. It is also quite easy to sow wherever there is spare space between other plants. Phacelia forms a fine, feathery carpet; it is deep-rooted, shades the soil, and lets the rain trickle through its well divided leaves. It is a good collector and retainer of dew, and makes a welcome splash of colour early in the year (see pages 85–90). Its flowering time is a long one and its scent fills the air, attracting butterflies and other insects which help to pollinate bushes and fruit-bearing plants. A very noteworthy point is the cloud of syrphus-flies which hover in the air over the phacelia area and then fly down onto the roses and certain other perennials to clear them of aphides and their eggs. If phacelia encourages these enemies of the aphis so much, then it is a real friend to the gardener. Once the plants have ceased blossoming, they make good compost material.

Sheet Composting
Whereas the above-mentioned preparatory crops (mustard, field beans etc.) are removed to make way for the tomatoes, late brassicas, cucumbers and so on that will follow, spinach is chopped down and left lying on top of its rows without further planting in them. The very early sowing of spinach as a protection for neighbouring plants against pests and to keep them shaded from too much sun, has high value for the garden right through the year; it also supplies spring greens and forms an essential part of the framework of rows on which our whole system is built up. When the spinach is cut down, the soft, quick-rotting root remains in the ground. In the past, little notice has been taken of the manure supplied by such root residues, because attention was concentrated on what the leaves were doing, but the method of companion planting with spinach, as with other plants, provides new perspectives.

Years of tests have shown that spinach is not only extraordinarily useful for

---

* Seeds are available from Wyartt Seeds (address given on page 125).

preparing the ground for the crops which are to follow, but they can be sown with great success under rose bushes or in the circular beds surrounding fruit trees. The beds are turned an attractive dark green by the spinach seedlings, and the spinach fertilizes the roses so well that they produce luxuriant blooms and green leaves which do not fall off prematurely. Spinach is good to sow under any kind of bush which does not need to have bare soil round it, but care must be taken to cut it down at the right time.

In mixed vegetable gardens, spinach makes a splendid foundation for composting on the soil surface. The leafy and very succulent plants lie in the spaces between the vegetables as the lowest layer of compost. Their leaves cover and shade the ground, and the earthworms gain extra nourishment too. All in all, the fertility of the soil is much improved.

The Forest Floor as an Example
If continual additions are made in the course of the year to the sheet compost, using all that the garden offers, the soil will profit from these valuable materials much more rapidly and surely than if they are fed to it via the more circuitous route of the compost heap. Compost heaps are never found in nature; at most, piles of leaves are formed which have drifted together under the action of the wind. Composting on the soil surface is the best imitation of what happens in nature and the often-quoted example of the woodlands illustrates this well; it is a real prototype for the use of sheet compost. The carpet of leaves and pine needles in a forest of mixed conifers and deciduous trees is constantly developing; it is moistened by the rain dripping from the branches, protected from the full glare of the sun, and enriched by animal droppings. The latter are the essential 'animal component' of the compost.

Suitable Materials
Decomposition of material into nutrients usable by plants takes place much more quickly and certainly in sheet composting than it does in compost heaps. The materials used should be just slightly wilted so as not to attract snails, but fresh enough to collect dew. Hence no straw or peat are used, but everything else that pertains to good, well made compost, and, when it is available, well rotted dung or some fertilizer of animal origin such as dried cow pats may be made full use of. A further layer could consist of medicinal herbs, followed by a layer from the outside leaves of lettuces or whatever is discarded when vegetables are harvested. Wild flowers can be added, plus dead flowers and hedge clippings at the end of the year. Always keep everything tidy by spreading grass or similar flat-lying material on top.

This covering then becomes a path which may be used at any time, even when the weather is wet. When necessary, the covering can be watered, and in fact this method saves water because it acts as a filter. The woods are again a good example of this, because the soil is never completely broken up by a downpour, owing to the roof of boughs and branches. The water is retained by the leaves to a certain extent and is dispensed to the plant community below, a little at a time.

Sources of Carbonic Acid for Plant Life
As has been remarked several times already, the soil is teeming with living creatures underneath the surface layer of compost. So what does all this mean for the prospective harvest? Plants construct their tissues, with the help of the energy derived from sunlight, out of water and the carbon dioxide contained in the air plus the minerals taken in through their roots from the soil. The process is a complicated one which can only be dealt with briefly here.

However, let us take another look at the source from which the carbon dioxide comes. It comes from the air, although its concentration there is low (only 0.03%). However, the plants have an additional source, the so-called 'soil-borne carbonic acid' which is liberated by the billions of tiny organisms in the soil. This carbonic acid comes from the vegetable matter we add to the earth for the benefit of its bacteria and from the leaves dropped by growing plants. It is a very useful supplement to the general supply. A substitute for this source of carbonic acid, which may be used in enclosed spaces such as greenhouses, is the direct addition of the acid. This has successfully improved growth, but is expensive and, above all, involves questions of dosage which do not arise when natural processes are utilized. It is obvious that the windshield provided by plants growing at different heights in companion culture gardens must help to conserve the carbon dioxide content of the soil.

Another virtue of the bacterial activity already mentioned is that it feeds the minerals required by plants into the soil solution. The mineral nutrients are liberated from the particles of earth into the soil water and are then taken up by the root hairs. Many cultivated plants live in close association with fungi and bacteria, through which they can make use of otherwise closed mineral sources. To sum up, surface composting ensures a constant supply of nutrients and water to the soil, gives it protection and enriches it in humus. The strips where the compost is laid down this year will become the places where vegetables are grown next year, since, as we have already stated, the rows are displaced 25 cm sideways. It will then be seen how plants growing in humus-rich soil have a higher resistance to pests and greater fecundity.

Soil Conditions
The nature of the soil varies quite considerably from garden to garden, and

every gardener thinks that his or her soil is 'particularly hard to work'. Soils differ from one another, for instance, in their lime content: they can be calcareous (alkaline) or deficient in lime (acid). According to their clay and sand content they are either heavy or light respectively. They contain different amounts of humus, and the ground itself is either level or sloping, protected from or exposed to the wind and so on.

All this influences the natural course of events and causes us to consider how we can mitigate unfavourable conditions or take advantage of favourable ones in some special way. Like the professional agriculturist or market gardener, the domestic gardener can have his soil analyzed. The results of the analysis will reveal which nutrients and essential elements are missing and the kinds and amounts of fertilizer that should be used.

As already mentioned, most gardeners and garden owners are dissatisfied with their soil when they first take it over or start to cultivate previously untilled land. However, although much may be done to improve the soil, it should be realized that it cannot be completely changed. When left to itself, it will gradually return to its original state after years of loving attention, because climatic and geological conditions inevitably lead in that direction. When under cultivation, it needs repeated attention along the same lines. Should the initial conditions be difficult, especially when the garden can offer no materials of its own to improve the soil, advantage may be taken of organic fertilizers on sale in the shops. If the soil is poor and sandy, and soil analysis has revealed a deficiency, the ground may be prepared initially with potash and phosphate fertilizers.

Clay soil will often look like that in the illustration opposite page 65, when it is not treated, i.e. when the humus content is not decisively increased and constantly made good. Nevertheless, the same soil can also look like that in the second picture: well broken up by roots, and full of earthworms. Given that a great many gardeners are unhappy with their soils, the question arises, what do some gardeners do to the land that is so wrong and disturbs it so much that it ceases to be productive and fruitful?

What is likely to damage the soil?
First there is the usual method of letting the ground lie fallow by digging it over in the autumn and leaving the bare earth exposed over the winter and until cultivation recommences in spring. In many gardens, nothing more is attempted until April, and summer sowings are left to do as best they may without any protection. Monoculture is a system that is much to blame here because the seedlings receive no shelter either from neighbouring plants or from any form of covering. Modern vineyards are typical examples of this since they suffer from

a loss of humus and actual erosion of the soil in bad weather. The soil is constantly at risk from rainstorms or when exposed to hours of fierce sunlight, because there is no subsidiary vegetation to hold it together or to shade it.

The ground may also be harmed by relentless human interference. The gardener is never happier than when hoeing, mowing and digging it up; but this meddling is senseless if the lifeless, lower layers are brought to the surface and the good humus, with which we have been presented during the year, is buried so deep that it is no longer available. The gardener can also do harm to the soil by trying to treat plant diseases with drastic remedies, and forgetting that true healing comes from the soil itself and is promoted by proper planting. The land can be adversely affected, too, if streams in the vicinity are diverted or dried up, and if trees and hedges are removed, in which case much of the gaseous exchange in the atmosphere disappears. It is also possible to overmanure, to manure at the wrong season and, of course, to manure with incorrect preparations – even when these are made from pure biological materials.

Harm can also be done using fresh dung, especially when it is in liquid form, thoroughly 'biological' though it may be! Rashly applied, liquid manure or slurry can kill the earthworms and, well-meaning though such treatment might appear, it could be a long time before the land recovers.

The application of cold, hard and chlorinated water can also damage the ground. Excess use of the hose or sprinkler is bad too, and not only damages the plants but hardens the soil. Market gardeners will confirm that such a practice tends to destroy the humus layer and that the ground becomes hard and cracked unless extra, large amounts of organic matter are worked into it.

Soil can be spoilt by walking on it, particularly in wet weather. This is especially true in spring – so do not tramp about the earth when it is soggy! Deferred sowing while the earth is drying out is compensated by quicker development of the plants. The seeds fall into fresh soft soil and are able to germinate and grow freely. No benefit will be reaped later in the year by sowing too early: if the soil is compacted in spring, it will still be hard and difficult in autumn. Nor should we overlook the danger to good soil structure represented by heavy equipment such as rotary hoes, particularly when used at the wrong time of year.

Finally, the soil can be spoilt by destroying the living creatures which inhabit it and are never useless but, as they interact with one another (coming and going, eating and being eaten), are very important for keeping the soil in good condition. This destruction of the soil's fauna can even occur when the gardener is doing his best to distinguish between pests and friendly organisms and is trying to exterminate the former while sparing the latter. More will be said about this in the section on animals in the garden.

It goes without saying that the organically-minded gardener will not employ chemical insecticides or weed killers. However, it may be that he will take over land that has been mistreated in this way by its previous owners with all the unfortunate consequences. He will then have to try to undo the damage by paying special attention to soil care in the years to come.

Heap Composting

In addition to composting on the soil surface which, because it imitates natural processes, gives optimum success in the shortest space of time, the compost heap or bin, is or was the gardener's best friend. Compost making is a speeded-up version of a maturing process that happens in Nature over a very long time, and sheet composting is the quickest and most immediate version of the process. Nevertheless, the compost heap still has its place in the garden. It can be used for all sorts of purposes, although it does have the disadvantage of encouraging weeds.

There is a lot of plant refuse that is not suitable for direct application as sheet compost: peahaulm, bulky vegetation, thin twigs etc. This should be set to one side at least until one has time to make a compost heap. A compost starter is helpful; all the same, it takes months to obtain the finished product.

The compost heap is a prime means of recycling the garden waste biologically, and its value is undisputed in maintaining the health of the land. However, sheet compost applied and made *in situ* is superior to compost taken from a heap. There are good reasons for this. The layer of sheet compost is in direct contact with the ground and undergoes the type of decomposition occurring in Nature without any loss of useful materials. It nourishes and creates a micro-climate for earthworms and countless lesser organisms. Each stage of decomposition takes place where the products are wanted and they are immediately available to form fresh soil.

In the following year, the plants spring up in unused and enriched soil, full of everything they need. The tilth is alive with activity and, since new materials of various kinds are continually being added, its surface is always topped with enough greenery to collect and store dew. This compost cover protects the ground from the hot sun and heavy rain and, if suitable plants are incorporated in it, it will help to drive away pests.

Such a ready-made compost offers great resistance to parasites during the following year, helping to get rid of nematodes and club root; it renews tired soil and forestalls degenerative tendencies.

Chopped Organic Material

This section will deal with a slightly different method of improving the soil. This is the preparation of organic materials, in which coarse and hard compost material is chopped or shredded by hand or by machine.

Composition
In the course of a gardening year, suitable material is collected as it becomes available and is broken up. It is chopped or shredded when fresh or slightly wilted, but before it starts to rot. Anything the garden supplies in the way of stems, twigs and brushwood can be used. The shredded mixture (which, like sheet compost or compost with rock powder, may also be enriched with organic manure of animal origin) has an addition of fresh green materials, e.g. newly-mown grass, to heat it up. This heating kills the seeds of weeds and, after a short time, when the heap has cooled down, it becomes the home of innumerable earthworms. To make the mixture a fertile and versatile one, certain wild flowers are added to it which are probably no longer found in the garden. Elder, which flourishes in chalky soil, can be chopped up at any stage of growth and provides the best defence there is against moles and voles.

Wild tansy (*Chrysanthemum vulgare*) and woodland fern leaves can be picked for their tendency to discourage pests and also supply extra potash. Other suggestions are yarrow (*Achillea millefolium*) and horse-tail (*Equisetum arvense*) and thin twigs of brier (*Rosa*). Oat straw is also useful if it can be obtained. All these things make the mixture light and loose. Perhaps the reader knows a friendly farmer who grows field beans (*Vicia faba*) – these have already been mentioned as a preparatory crop – and can beg the bean haulm from him in autumn. Bean haulm contains protein, is very soft and rots down quickly. It forms a good additive.

Because so many plants are used which are inimical to pests, no snails and hardly any other undesirable creatures are found in this compost. The rather coarse nature of the main ingredients discourages them too. The plants on which this compost is used grow to be strong and healthy-looking.

The shredded mixture for covering the soil of woodland plants such as strawberries, raspberries and of course roses, should contain green twigs from conifers, i.e. woodland materials for woodland plants. Obviously, woodland-type organic material should not be restricted to conifer twigs, but these should be mixed with the materials already mentioned.

The woody bits and pieces mixed into the heap, e.g. the side shoots of wild roses, thick and thin twigs and chips of different kinds of wood all contain lignin, which can inhibit plant growth. Therefore, the bulk of this woody material must occupy a special heap reserved for use on such plants as roses, strawberries and raspberries; in other words, on plants whose natural habitat is the forest. Some wood, however, may be incorporated in any shredded organic material. This can usefully be spread like ordinary sheet compost to inhibit the germination of weeds. As the organic material is in the process of rotting down, small pieces of wood mixed in here and there will do much to improve the texture of the soil by the following spring. The systematic gardener will make a note of the exact composition of the different heaps of shredded material, so that the best mixture can be spread around each type of plant.

Use
This organic material which has been chopped, shredded or otherwise broken up, and put in a pile where it is allowed to heat up and then cool down, is spread on the soil as required during the course of the year; in kitchen gardens, this will be where the spinach, the vegetable refuse and the wild flowers have already been strewn.

In autumn or towards the end of summer, more chopped materials are heaped up where they will be needed later (for the round beds around trees, for beds of roses or lilies, for strawberry and raspberry beds), and also in places where no sowing will be done in spring. As the weather begins to improve at the beginning of the year, the materials will start to decay and will give the growing plants both nourishment and protection. These last-made heaps of shredded organic material will heat up right into late autumn, so there is no fear that they will become a breeding ground for weeds. If, as may happen, weeds are found during the spring in lily or iris beds which were covered with shredded organic matter in autumn, they are easy to pull from soil made loose by this 'compost', even when they are as troublesome as ground elder.

Due to its great value, both as protection and fertilizer, shredded organic material is also good for many pot plants. When it is used for them, there is no need to leave a watering space in the pot or tub, because the water will not slop over but will gradually sink down through the protective covering. This is especially important for plants kept over the winter, since not only is the water well retained but it dissolves nutrients as it slowly percolates. A glance at the leaves of the plants concerned will reveal that they are unusually fresh and green.

Shredded organic material must not be used on seed rows but only around plants which are *already rooted*, and nothing should be sown, planted or pricked out in it. For instance, it must not be put into a hole dug for a rose bush. Let it be emphasized that ripe compost, which has been carefully turned every now and again and is sieveable and suitable for seed drills, must never be exchanged for the shredded organic material. Valuable as the latter is, it is only 'compost in the making'. In the following year, however, the gardener will reap the benefit from it throughout the garden and in every plant to which it has been applied.

Contribution of Shredded Organic Material to Soil Health
As this 'compost' does so much for the plants in a mixed garden, (giving them nutrients plus shelter and protection), it is extraordinarily beneficial. The shredded covering material decays thoroughly, evenly and quickly, so that within a short time it has given rise to humus-rich soil. Never is plant health so conspicuous, never are yields so good as when the land is covered with this finely broken up organic material.

The chapter on herbs supplies additional information on the health-promoting and pest-inhibiting properties of the individual species. Wormwood (*Artemisia absinthium*) and sage (*Salvia officinalis*) are protective plants, stinging-nettles, with their high content of silicic acid, make good fertilizer and ward off many destructive influences, and so on. We already know about the way in which mustard repels nematodes and how the onion prevents fungal attacks. All these useful properties are incorporated in good chopped organic material to be applied direct to the garden where it is required. The question is often asked whether mice are attracted by the litter of leaves; the answer is no, especially when elder is employed in the mixture. Our gardening should always be planned with one eye on the intrinsic value of the plants, so that advantage may be taken, one way or another, of everything the garden itself provides.

Encouraging Earthworms in the Garden
Anyone who undertakes companion planting as described here will soon notice a striking increase in the number of earthworms in the soil. This is due to the plentiful year-round supply of foodstuffs. Many readers will probably have wondered why no mention has been made of kitchen waste in connection with compost since, in theory, refuse that will rot down can be separated from that which will not and can then be tipped over the sheet compost. This would be good for the earthworms but not quite so good in other respects. Experience has shown that other animals which occupy the garden (including dogs and cats) will forage in it for what they can eat. They paw the ground, make everything untidy and do a great deal of damage.

The right way to go about things is to put kitchen waste and similar materials which will rot in a compost heap of their own, keeping it carefully covered. If this compost heap is placed where the refuse can be easily added to it in any weather and at any time of year, it will soon become full of earthworms which freely multiply in the generous food supply. The rich mixture of earthworms and earth can now be used in the garden at intervals, either by spreading it direct on the rows covered with sheet compost (which will soon be processed by invading earthworms), or by adding it to the slightly warm heap of chopped organic material. For parks and allotments which are not near the house, earthworm containers are available. When they are emptied, some of the worms must be left behind to keep the process going when more compost material is added. It need hardly be said that the containers must not be kept indoors and should be well covered.

Covering this earthworm compost (or, in general, the place where kitchen waste is tipped and where earthworms quickly congregate) is not simply a matter of tidiness. The covering ought to be dark and fairly thick. Darkness, warmth and damp are necessary both for the earthworms themselves and for the things on which they feed, encouraging them to breed prolifically. Air and moisture can enter the open sides of a small heap.

Although the earthworms multiply quickly in this soft nutrient-rich mixture, the gardener who is restricted to breeding them in containers will have to do without the small creatures such as woodlice and centipedes which invariably accompany earthworms in the open and share so much of the work of compost preparation. Earthworms travel far and wide and soon find their way into compost heaps and surface compost, but introducing them in quantity at an early stage reduces the decomposition time in a way that is almost indispensable.

The particular variety of earthworm most suitable for gardening purposes is the red *Eisenia foetida*, which has an excellent reputation for producing compost from waste matter. However, the compost made by worms from household scraps has only a limited use in the garden. It has its place – as already indicated – but solely as an 'inoculation' for shredded sheet compost. 'Red worm compost' should never be put on seed or plant beds. In accurate tests it has yielded negative results for germination (which is inhibited) for liability to disease and infestation, and for vegetable quality (which is coarsened) – all signs of overmanuring.

While on the subject of earthworms, we may as well dispose of the assertions occasionally made that worms can turn into pests and start devouring living roots. This is completely untrue. The large earthworm (*Lumbricus terrestris*), which is ubiquitous in garden and field, is our most useful assistant in working the soil. Its excrement, which is full of nutrients, has no deleterious effects of any sort. The earthworm never eats fresh, living roots, or indeed any healthy, living plant tissues. It presents us with well ventilated, nutrient-rich, nicely sifted soil, and so does the land nothing but good. Both types of earthworm mentioned are necessary, and the gardener should do his best to increase his stock of them.

Water and Watering

A piece of advice was offered in the Introduction to the effect that the gardener should spare the soil and squander its resources as little as possible. The same advice applies to water. Every plant requires water for its growth. Compost requires water too, while it is being made, although the rain is usually sufficient here. Normally, our flowers and vegetables will get enough moisture from the rainwater that is stored in the compost and in the soil beneath it and this remains available over a long period. If sheet compost is well made, it will also collect dew as an additional source of supply.

Nevertheless, there are many occasions when we are glad to be able to water our plants. I say advisedly, 'water', not 'drench', and certainly not 'sprinkle'. If watering has to be done, it should be done over the surface compost, which will serve as a filter. Care should be taken never to pour water on the plants direct and especially never on their leaves as this will encourage fungal diseases! Besides, plants absorb water through their rootlets, which form a fine network just under the soil, rather than through their tap-roots (if they have them).

Since we have had to do our gardening in dry years as well as wet ones, we have been able to make accurate observations. It is sufficient to water the sheet compost. If the garden hose is laid on the covering of compost to create a moist environment for the plants slowly and gradually, this will be quite helpful.

Wandering round with a watering can is very tiring and it is difficult to keep the water off the leaves of the plants. Wetting the leaves definitely encourages many diseases (including mildew). Sprinkler irrigation is out of place in a biological garden. It is exactly the reverse of what nature does for us. The action of rain-water is different from that of tap-water, and tap-water can never replace rain-water.

If it is possible for the gardener to collect rain-water, he will be providing something especially beneficial for his plants. Generally speaking, however, one has to be satisfied with what the waterworks supplies. It goes without saying that water is needed by all mature plants, and is also necessary for preparing liquid manures from plant materials. Water should not be used on seed drills or beds. This practice is based on the idea that the seeds will find it easier to germinate; however, it is better and more correct to sow the seeds at varying depths according to their size, to cover them well, and to let the soil look after them without further interference. Watering the earth every now and again stimulates the growth of the seeds, but unless we can be sure of persevering with it, it is far preferable to trust nature and wait for them to germinate under the influence of rain and the natural humidity of the air.

Parsley is an example of a plant that is reluctant to germinate, and will often keep the gardener waiting. Nevertheless, it causes no problems when the ripe seeds fall of their own accord and are allowed to rest peacefully in the ground until ready. A single shower is not enough; the air and the soil must be damp at the same time.

Our observations on this score have been confirmed by such biennials as campanula, wallflowers (*Cheiranthus cheiri*), pansies (*Viola tricolor*) and others, the heads of which may be laid on the dry earth with their ripe seeds. The seeds will always germinate without a single watering, or rather *because* they have not once been watered. When they are not given water, the plants grow without interruption and the sensitive seedlings do not die.

An economical use of water that nevertheless ensures that the plants are adequately supplied, is very much dependent on correct composting, preparatory sowing and combined sowing, as these things help the soil to retain moisture. When making use of 'unwatered' seed drills, as exemplified by the biennials mentioned above, the organically-minded gardener will welcome the wild flowers which spring up beside them, because they provide shade and retain moisture, and he will allow them to stay where they are until they become big enough to make a nuisance of themselves.

3.
Garden Weeds

The boundary between herbs and weeds is indistinct. Although the term 'weeds' is generally used, it is best to think of them as 'wild flowers', since they enjoy such a close and important relationship with the soil.

What are Weeds?
Generally speaking, weeds are regarded as a nuisance and are rooted out as quickly as possible. Yet nothing in nature is without its use, and perhaps we should be asking ourselves what benefit they are in the garden.

All the rows have been cultivated for the first time. Some of the lettuces and radishes have already been pulled. The cabbage lettuce, young beetroot, carrots, spring onions and kohlrabi will shortly be ready. All the free spaces are covered and can be used as paths. As the crops are removed, the land is freshly tilled as part of a continual process.

Below left:
Aphides on rosebuds.

Below right:
These roses now bloom free of aphides. At the time when these pictures were taken, pests of various sorts made their appearance in the garden. Although the companion-planted garden was relatively free from them, some roses showed clear signs of infestation. Ladybirds arrived at the same time as the aphides and a few days later healthy roses came into bloom. Further conditions for success are to work the soil under the standard roses with a fork, to keep it well watered and to fertilize it with an undiluted liquid manure made from stinging-nettles (see page 53).

1. Weeds are first and foremost plants which establish a place for themselves before man sows a single seed.

2. Weeds are plants which always occur in plant communities, never in 'monoculture'.

3. Weeds always grow where they will find what they need and where their living conditions are fulfilled.

4. Weeds are plants which are healthiest in the place they have chosen for themselves, have an indomitable will to live, are very aggressive and make use of all the opportunities they can find for growth, reproduction and survival. They can not be compelled to grow in a different environment or at another time of year. If a plant fits this description, we call it a 'weed'.

Nowadays, there are gardens in which weeds no longer grow because their owners have used every available means to eradicate them. It goes without saying that these are not biologically and ecologically balanced gardens in the sense intended in this book.

Top left:
Half-grown tomatoes undersown with mustard, next to spreading vegetables (courgettes or cucumbers) – no conflict over space requirements here!

Below left:
Carefully arranged rows of other vegetables. In the intermediate spaces lies spinach that has been chopped down; its roots are rotting in the ground. The spinach is covered with grass, the outside leaves of lettuces and cabbages and other quick-decomposing organic materials. This inhibits weeds and feeds the earthworms.

Top right:
Rows of two kinds of brassicas separated by celeriac. The cabbage rows had field beans as a preparatory crop – sown deep and very early. This has given a slow-working but optimum supply of nitrogen. The soil is covered at the side and two bean plants which were left standing by mistake are also still visible.

Below right:
The peas to the left of the lettuce help to improve the soil and increase its nitrogen content. These make 'good neighbours'.

The Function of Weeds

Weeds, or better 'wild flowers', usually have healing properties. They widen the range provided by cultivated plants and increase the companion planting potential. They impart their healing virtues to the soil and to the plants growing in it. The idea that all living things play their part is very true of the wild flowers growing in our gardens.

Out in the countryside there are more wild flowers than can easily be counted. Many of them possess a high pharmaceutical value which can help to preserve health and heal diseases. All the wild flowers of field and meadow which are useful to man, could also be gracing our gardens, at least in so far as we can make use of them and they do not get out of hand. Wild flowers benefit not only farmland and indeed the soil underlying the whole landscape, but the soil of smaller plots of land too. Many of the garden's weeds, i.e. wild flowers, contain known active principles which would do much to improve the land if only they were utilized and gardening were made fully 'biological'.

Weeds as Soil Indicators

Some weeds are true soil indicators, and their presence will often reveal the nature of the soil together with any deficiencies from which it may be suffering. There is no space to go into details here, except for one or two hints to point the reader in the right direction.

Broadly speaking, there are quite a number of wild flowers which indicate whether the soil is limy, deficient in lime or acid, and by taking notice of them many a set-back in planning and planting gardens could be avoided. In an old garden, one knows from experience which weeds to expect and where to look for them; yet every spring some new and perhaps completely different species may arrive, and any such change could tell us something we ought to know about the state of our land. Therefore it is wise to leave the so-called weeds alone at first, at least until they can be identified.

For example, the harebell (or bluebell of Scotland), pheasant's eye (*Adonis vernalis*) and larkspur (*Delphinium*) show that the soil is not only limy but also well supplied with humus. In other words it is fertile. If, on this calcareous soil, charlock (*Sinapis arvensis*), red poppy (*Papaver rhoeas*) (slightly poisonous), dead-nettle (*Lamiastrum*), lesser bindweed (*Convolvulus*) and speedwell (*Veronica*) (which has been greatly on the increase in recent years) also grow, a *deep*, fertile soil is indicated. When stinging-nettles, black nightshade (*Solanum nigrum*) (another poisonous plant) and fumitory are to be seen, the soil is nitrogenous with plenty of iron; however, since the soils in which these grow can be weakly acid, these plants are not lime indicators. The arrival of the small annual stinging-nettle, signals a very nitrogenous soil, full of humus and nutrients but possibly overmanured. The gardener should make a note of the place where these weeds congregate (say at the base of some bush) so that he can avoid putting nitrogenous fertilizers there until the excess nitrogen has been used up.

Orach (*Atriplex patula*), foxtail (*Amaranthus retroflexus*) and cock's foot (*Ranunculus*) are signs of a heavy but not dry soil, but if cock's foot is joined by goose-grass (*Potentilla anserina*), cornmint (*Mentha arvensis*), knot-grass (*Polyganum*) coltsfoot (*Tussilago*) or horsetail (*Equisetum arvense*) the ground will be found to be waterlogged and poorly ventilated. A knowledgeable farmer might shake his head and say, 'We shan't be able to do much with the land until it's drained,' but gardeners are able to overcome this by planting suitable flowers in this type of soil. Considerable success can be obtained by putting in water-iris (*Iris pseudacorus*) where the above-mentioned weeds have been flourishing, even when the water present is not actually visible.

The list of wild flowers which are good for the garden is endless, and it is advisable to find out in spring what is growing and where it is growing so that we can form a considered opinion. Special mention should be made of two wild flowers regarded as particularly troublesome garden weeds: ivy-leaved speedwell (*Veronica hederaefolia*) and grey field speedwell (*Veronica polita*). Chick-weed (*Stellaria media*) and speedwell are infallible indicators of soil with a very high humus and nutrient content, and in particular a high content of nitrogen, so it is not surprising that they tend to spring up in the compost we spread over our seed rows or on our strawberry beds.

Asset Plants
Some of our wild flowers are real assets. Among them are ground ivy (*Glechoma hederacea*), dead-nettle, bugle (*Ajuga*), mint (*Mentha*) and purslane (*Portulaca*). When they spring up in the round beds around trees, they afford useful shade to the ground, and help to ward off pests. The stinging-nettle is especially valuable. It supplies iron, silicic acid and a great number of trace elements; when removed, it leaves behind a humus-rich soil. Many of these so-called weeds are favourite haunts of bees which are attracted to them early in the year at a time when other plants are not yet in bloom. Therefore, it would be foolish to root out these plants before others are in flower for the bees to visit. (Since it is true that for every garden pest there grows a remedy, these helpers should be left alone to get on with their job).

However, some wild flowers help indirectly as well as directly, due to the presence of small amounts of toxins which are important for many small creatures in the garden. Such spring flowers as the crocus (*Crocus*) and snowdrop (*Galanthus nivalis*) are among those which contain these important traces of poison.

A Biological Cycle

I have tried to show how the biological cycle which is so often disturbed can still be put right when all forms of garden life are allowed to play their part. To give an example: the birds living in our garden, the blackbirds, thrushes, finches, tits, redstarts and many others, absorb these minute amounts of poison which they need to supplement their diet for the good of their health. They know instinctively which plants will give them what they need. It is these birds which are our earliest pest-fighters. They sit on every branch pecking at what to us are noxious grubs and insects and to them are full of protein for their fledgelings. This first link in the chain will give the reader some idea of how the biological cycle runs.

In spite of the annoyance caused by garden weeds, the gardener should be prepared to put up with them until they become a real nuisance. Nevertheless, the vegetable patch must be kept free of weeds and so must the ground around the roses, irises and other displays.

Wild Flowers and Butterflies

If wild flowers are tolerated in the garden, butterflies are sure to appear sooner or later. Weeds are the food plants of many butterflies and their caterpillars, and as such are responsible for their preservation and dissemination. Obviously, the gardener does not want to see weeds springing up in the middle of the garden, but all gardens have edges where wild flowers can be accommodated as places of refuge for these beautiful creatures. The most suitable flowers are the stinging-nettle, thistle (*Carduus*), dead-nettle, violet (*Viola*), plantain (*Plantago*), willow-herb (*Epilobium angustifolium*) and species of spurge (*Euphorbia*). On running through the names of these plants, it becomes obvious that no part of the ground will be left unused by them.

Naturally, some of our regular garden plants will serve as a back-up, plants such as the hazelnut bush and birch tree (*Betula*), the privet (*Liguster*) and the lilac (*Syringa*).

Which butterflies and moths are linked with special plants? The emperor moth favours blackberry, rose, sloe (*Prunus spinesa*), plantain, great mullein (*Verbascum*) and elder (*Sambucus nigra*), for example. Other species to be found in our many gardens are: the cabbage white, which easily becomes a pest if the proper companion planting methods are not employed, vanessa, which is perfectly harmless, the small tortoise-shell, which likes to lay its eggs on the nasturtium (*Tropaeolum*) but does only superficial damage, the red admiral, the brimstone butterfly and the painted lady, which lay their eggs almost exclusively on the stinging-nettle. When these insects are flying about and adding a delicate splash of colour to the scene, they will often be observed in the vicinity of single dahlias, Michaelmas daisies, lavender (*Lavandula angusti-folia*) and honeysuckle (*Lonicera*), that is to say near all those traditional plants that enhance the cottage garden effect of the particular plot of land.

Fertilizers from Wild Plants and their Action

Anyone whose main aim until now has been the creation of a weed-free garden may be regretting, now that he knows their value, that he has so few of them. One of their great uses, for example is in the preparation of liquid manures.

The stinging-nettle is really indispensable for this purpose. This plant, aptly called the richest weed (which in fact it is) is particularly important in sheet compost layers. In addition, the nettle's stinging hairs discourage snails. Stinging-nettles collect and retain dew and a row of vegetables never looks better and healthier than when the plants are growing in nettle compost. The nettle is the basic ingredient in all those manures which are also required as a form of pest control.

Comfrey (*Symphytum asperum*) which is planted as a medicinal herb, for its decorative appearance and to encourage bees, makes good covering material and is suitable for chopped and other types of compost, besides making very good liquid fertilizer! Liquid comfrey fertilizer is milder than the stinging-nettle variety, does not have such a penetrating smell, and feeds and promotes the growth and flowering of all pot, tub-grown and outdoor plants. Comfrey fertilizer is slower-acting but is very suitable for mixing with stinging-nettle fertilizer. The two plants can be processed together or the ready-made liquids can be stirred into one another. Since the main purpose here is to manure the ground, the leaves of the dandelion (*Taraxacum officinale*), cow parsnip (*Heracleum*), plantain, yarrow and other roadside weeds may usefully be added to the preparation. Comfrey is a plant that has become forgotten in this century – a fate shared by many traditional herbs. The man in the street would be at a loss to describe it. Just now, however, it is arousing fresh interest as a 'rediscovered' herb. The fact that a number of distinct varieties are available should not confuse the gardener, for whom they all have the same value, whether they are native to us or are exotic imports. The normal habitat of the native variety (*Symphytum officinale* belonging to the Boraginaceae) is to be found in damp places near streams and rivers as it likes wet, or at least moist, nitrogenous ground. Its names – knitbone, boneset or blackwort – refer to its healing action in extracts and ointments. It is debatable whether or not it should be taken internally and, with so many edible things growing in the garden, there is no need to try the experiment. Its value for external application and for the garden itself has been proved beyond doubt.

Where comfrey was once grown for fodder (as far back as the beginning of this century), specimens may still be found over a wide area and are easy to gather for the garden. Reproduction is either vegetative from pieces of root or through the seeds, which are dispersed by small animals without any assistance from the gardener. Comfrey is known as a herbaceous plant; it can live for several years, but will disappear if the light conditions and the conditions of the soil alter, or when a cutting is taken at the wrong time (even though several cuttings a year may be safely taken from mature plants). Nevertheless, the roots of this plant spread so efficiently that it is bound to reappear at some time.

The elder is another wild plant deserving mention; it is common in regions with chalky soil and has many useful properties, among them the fact that it discourages mice, voles and moles. With moles, I find it is sufficient to stick a few twigs in the molehill or to make a border of twigs round our cold-frames. For gardening purposes, elder is used at the time the sap is rising. All parts of the elder are employed, leaves, twigs and fruit-bearing branches, and these are either put down as a covering to protect the neighbouring plants from flea-beetles, or else made into a liquid which is especially potent against animal pests.

Horsetail and tansy are two plants which are sometimes found growing wild and are sometimes seen growing 'uninvited' in the garden. They make particularly good 'brews' with which to water other plants and both can be liquefied to make a fertilizer. This liquid helps to prevent fungal attacks on strawberries, tomatoes and onions when there is mildew about. It is also good for seedlings suffering from 'damping-off' disease through being planted in soil that is too warm and damp and too rich in nutrients. Horsetail liquid combats rust in celery and celeriac. The young plants are placed in the ready-made fluid for a few hours before being planted out. A combination of horsetail and stinging-nettle liquids is favourable in this case. Mallows (*Malva silvestris*) (including hollyhocks) tend to suffer from rust when the air is not sufficiently damp. When they are young they should be given a foliar spray with horsetail liquid several times.

Valerian (*Valeriana officinalis*), which may be found growing on walls and on the outskirts of woods, is given in the form of an infusion or fermented liquid to all flowering and fruiting plants, including beans, peas, tomatoes, cucumbers and courgettes. However, valerian liquid is not used on lettuces, carrots or onions. It is mild but potent. This is especially evident when it is given to such plants as roses and irises, which will then bloom as never before. Valerian liquid is best used early, and will then produce exceptional results.

Wild flowers can obviously prove very helpful in any garden, big or small. What is more, the residues at the bottom of the vats of liquid 'weed manure' make as good a compost starter as one could wish to find.

4.
Medicinal Herbs and Culinary Plants

Can culinary herbs also promote the health of the garden? We can no longer overlook the medicinal and culinary uses of herbs as far as diet is concerned. These plants look after bodily health, help to develop, strengthen and protect the organs, and provide the body with endurance and vitality; in addition, they can replace much of the goodness which is absent in denatured foodstuffs. Although this has been known for many years, what has not been known but has only recently been discovered, bit by bit, is the great value of these plants to the garden; their particular uses are in preparing the soil, keeping it in good condition, and in nourishing and protecting other plants.

To make the garden permanently healthy, herbs should be included in the garden plan and should be seen as an integral part of cultivation. Although many herbs have many properties in common, such as an abundance of vitamins, some have specific properties which we would do well to utilize.

Growing Herbs as Part of the Companion-planting System
When sown, planted or bedded out in the right place, herbs, like vegetables, can make good neighbours for other plants. They can protect against pests and can help to check diseases. When reduced to liquid fertilizer, they are excellent for manuring and improving the soil. Herbs make a good ground cover when they are placed under and around other plants. They enhance the beneficial effect both of sheet compost and compost taken from the bin.

Because they are so salutary, the following herbs are worth mentioning: members of the onion family (especially garlic), also mustard – an ancient, biblical herb of healing; nasturtium, garden-cress, watercress and last but not least marigold (*Calendula*), the healing properties of which have been known since the twelfth century. The petals of this flower are made into a sovereign ointment even today. There is no need to worry about where to plant the stinging-nettle, since it will be only too happy to plant itself, but finding the right niches for the other herbs may require a little thought.

Annuals

Annual herbs do not need their own patch of ground and certainly not their own beds (in our garden, we have done away with beds in any case); nor do they need their own rows, but are scattered among rows of more regularly spaced plants to help them and to protect them. (This method applies to all annual herbs.) These herbs are well known for their use in the kitchen and they should be readily available early in the year.

Dill (*Anethum graveolens*) is particularly suitable for companion sowing in spring and should be placed in every row of carrots. The dill and carrot seeds germinate together and give each other mutual support as they grow. All herbs secrete valuable chemicals, as do vegetables, above and below ground; the valuable substances secreted by dill go a long way to keeping neighbouring plants healthy. This is true when dill is sown with cucumbers for example (see the illustration facing page 64), with all members of the cabbage family, with beetroot and with many other vegetables. Because dill is even richer in vitamins than parsley (*Carum petroselinium*) or paprika, it is an especially important herb in the kitchen. The whole plant may be used, including the root, stalk and seeds. Dill is also valuable in the garden because, as an early grower, it provides welcome shade for later plants. The gardener will be well advised to add dill to every subsequent sowing and then there will be a constant supply of the fresh young herb for kitchen use.

Chervil (*Anthriscus cerefolium*) is another herb that should be sown early for the pot. This old medicinal herb, which is packed with vitamin C, is good for purifying the blood in spring as it tends to remove waste products from the body. No difficulty is encountered in raising chervil in the garden as an accompaniment to every fresh sowing of lettuce. One can begin early in the year, sowing it with lettuces and endives, and continue sowing, returning to the first-sown row of chervil, allowing it to stay green over the winter ready to grow again in spring. In other words, we can have chervil freely available at all times. What use is chervil in the garden? It protects lettuces with which it is sown from greenfly, mildew and snails, and keeps them tender for a long time. The rather pungent smell also discourages ants.

Summer savory (*Satureja hortensis*) is another annual that does not need a place of its own but is put in with other plants. Since it is sensitive to frost, it should not be sown until the middle of May, when it is best combined with beans. These are then kept free from aphides, including the black bean aphis. When it is picked, the root is left to rot in the ground so that the latter may benefit from its essential chemical contents.

Basil (*Ocimum basilicum*) is an unpretentious herb that has been called 'the queen of spices'. This is another plant which has to be sown late; it is the natural companion of other late crops such as cucumbers, courgettes and fennel (*Foeniculum vulgare*), all of which are sensitive to frost. In fact, we are first made aware that summer is departing when the leaves of the basil begin to turn brown. Cucumber plants growing near basil remain healthy for a long time, do not suffer from early mildew and yield well. Since basil is very attractive to bees, the cucumbers, which also rely on insects for fertilization, benefit too.

Borage (*Borago officinalis*) a nervine and blood-purifier is found in almost every garden and does the garden as much good as it does the gardener. When sown as an auxiliary crop during the growing season, borage has proved itself to be extraordinarily effective against pests in kohlrabi and all other types of brassica, which are kept completely free from attack until late in the year. Borage leaves are so hairy that snails do not like touching them. In our garden, we keep picking the leaves and do not allow the borage growing in the vegetable rows to flower lest it becomes too dominant. However, the garden has many places for it to spring up of its own accord, thereby providing the benefit of its soil-penetrating power. This important property is particularly useful in heavy or hard ground. There is nothing like borage for loosening the soil in a helpful manner.

The empty spaces between strawberry plants are best used for sowing mustard (*Sinapis alba*). It always appears and it has recently been recognized that it wards off nematodes. This sowing of mustard to accompany strawberries is best done after picking and cleaning the rows, that is to say after the leaves have been cut off, the weeds have been removed and the soil has been loosened. This is the right time to sow mustard which grows quickly and protects the strawberries. As winter draws on, it disintegrates into the soil.

Marigolds can also be used for planting with strawberries (see page 55), mustard and marigold are not normally viewed as medicinal herbs, but do have some use in the kitchen. The orange-yellow petals of marigold ought to be used more often than in the past, as should mustard seedlings. It is important to cut the mustard when it is young and at the same stage of growth at which we cut garden-cress. It then has a similar value and effect to the latter, although it is nothing like as pungent.

Parsley is another good secondary plant to put in with certain types of vegetable. It is indispensable in cookery because of its many different vitamins and other active ingredients, and should be used regularly but in moderation. It is a good protective plant but has properties that make it a difficult partner. Borders are the best position for parsley if it has stable neighbours. It makes a good partner for the sturdy onion and, above all, for tomatoes. Pests will not attack it or the plants beside it, but it is susceptible to disease. Parsley should never be put next to a weak partner; young lettuce, for example, would begin to die after it was half grown.

Marigolds, too, are valuable culinary plants as already mentioned. Their big root system gives them a special value in the garden, and they are ideal for planting under tomatoes, the surplus plants being used as a soil covering; however, *Calendula* is very beneficial anywhere, both for the soil and as a 'good neighbour' to main crops generally.

Among the annuals are onions and their relatives garlic, leeks and chives. All these varieties of onion are to be prized, not only for the zest they bring to cooking and for their health-giving properties, but as indispensable plants for warding off mould. All we have to decide is the best place to put them, knowing that wherever we plant them they will have a strong influence. Garlic is especially suitable for keeping mice away from roses and lilies etc. Strawberries, which are so susceptible to attacks by nematodes and mould, are in particular need of the help of these vegetables, and we should always remember not to plant this fruit by itself but to mix it with some of the onion tribe (see illustration of leeks growing between strawberries, page 16).

Garden-cress is a healing herb with a very pronounced action. Spring is one of the best times of year to eat it, as this is the time when people generally suffer from a lack of vitamins. Its action in the garden is very aggressive and its use as a neighbour for other plants is limited. Thus there is no place for it in the vegetable patch, but if planted at the base of trees, it will keep the aphides away. Marigolds, nasturtium and *Tagetes* can also be planted around trees as protective plants.

Annuals have yet another use without there being any call for them to have a place of their own in the garden (see the introduction to this section on page 56). They can shade and improve the soil, helping it to retain water and breaking it up with their roots. Mustard has already been mentioned and is worth remembering again at this point. It has very practical advantages and, if it is cut down when still tender, the residue will cause no trouble.

A preparatory sowing of celery (*Apium graveolens*) is very effective for controlling caterpillars and flea-beetles in cabbages. It should be sown in rows with the late cabbage plants. The celery left standing between the brassicas will also protect them from the cabbage white butterfly. After the brassicas have been cut, the celery is left to see the winter through and to be ready for cutting again in spring.

All the herbs mentioned above have great value as 'good neighbour plants', and the organically-minded gardener would do well not to ignore them.

Perennials

Something must now be said about the more shrubby, perennial herbs. Thinking back to the annual herbs described above, it will be realized that not one of them can be given up. The perennials, however, are not so indispensable, especially for the beginner. There is no rule that perennials (with all their fine qualities as supporting plants to main crops) have to be grown in beds of their own, although they do have to be bedded out. With some, the plants can be raised the same year, but others should be sown in spring and then thinned out for planting out in autumn. They are subsequently no trouble, remain crisp, and definitely require no fertilizer (even fertilizer of the biological kind). Perennials contain especially valuable substances – scents, oils and secretions – which can help other crops. The relative amount of these substances is reduced when the plants stand in fertile soil that has been overmanured. All of them are aromatic and are therefore defence plants. In the garden, they do wonders for the environment, since their perfumes pervade the air. Like the wild flowers, they all attract bees. Their names are familiar to everybody:

Cummin (*Carum carvi*) and coriander (*Coriandrum sativum*)
Lavender and rue (*Ruta graveolens*)
Rosemary (*Rosmarinus officinalis*) and sage
Hyssop (*Hyssopus officinalis*) and thyme (*Thymus vulgaris*)
Salad burnet (*Sanguisorba minor*) and lovage (*Levisticum officinale*)
Mugwort (*Artemisia vulgaris*) and balm (*Melissa officinalis*)
Chives and costmary (*Chrysanthemum balsamita*)
Sorrel (*Rumex acetosa*) and tarragon (*Artemisia dracunculus*)
Wormwood (*Artemisia absinthium*) and valerian

The question now is, where are these perennials to be bedded out when ready? Also, which plants are most useful, what effects do they have and what is the best position for them? The last pair mentioned above are quite exceptional.

Wormwood should always be put in by itself, so that there is no risk of it being mistaken for mugwort in the kitchen. Wormwood has a very high defence value, but it is not kind to the soil. Earthworms vacate the soil in which it is standing – therefore it must not be used in compost! The place for wormwood is, without doubt, next to the currant bushes, especially the black currants, so susceptible to rust. (Wormwood is the only known biological preventive of rust disease.) The place where wormwood has been sown or raised can be recognized years later, since the growth of other nearby plants is inhibited by the same poisonous secretions which make it such a good defence against rust. It may also be cut up and laid on affected cabbage plants when celery is not doing enough to help.

Valerian, which is the second plant holding an exceptional position, is used in the garden simply as an infusion of the blossom to stimulate fruiting vegetables. It is the garden's own flowering promoter and, naturally, profuse flowering (when properly controlled) promises a rich harvest.

Other Suggested Perennials

Since perennials – in contrast to annuals – cannot be incorporated with the main vegetables in the general scheme of mixed cropping, a few hints regarding their planting and use will be in order here.

Pride of place belongs to lavender with its double action of flower and leaf. It should be planted wherever ants are a nuisance as they always give lavender a wide berth. What ants do in the garden is generally not known and something will be said about them later (see page 73). Lavender goes well with all bushes, especially rose bushes, because it discourages aphides. In the kitchen, a small green sprig of lavender (and the same applies to some other herbs) is used as an additive to heavy meals. Lavender has a beneficial effect on the glands, and is cholagogic (promoting the flow of bile) and tranquillizing. Both the flowers and the leaves have cosmetic applications, and are used in the linen press and the wardrobe to drive away moths. It is recommended for 'household use'.

Lavender is interchangeable with rosemary in the kitchen. The latter is sensitive to frost however, and so it is a good idea to have plenty of lavender available for those occasions when there is a shortage of rosemary. Rosemary can be left out in the garden during the summer, but is best kept potted when set out between the roses and other bushes, so that it can easily be brought indoors for the winter* Lavender and rosemary are interchangeable in use, but as lavender is no trouble in the garden, it is more useful generally. As will be recalled, butterflies are dependent on many plants. Lavender is a veritable landing platform for these beautiful creatures and has no rival for attracting them in number and variety.

An important perennial medicinal and pot herb is sage, an ancient garden plant. In the list of herbs (see page 117), some details are given on its action and on its uses in the kitchen. Hyssop and thyme also deserve mention with sage. These three plants have a similar effect on the garden. They definitely stop infestations with caterpillars, especially those of the cabbage white butterfly. Unfortunately, the vegetable bed is no place for hyssop, thyme and sage, simply because they *are* perennials. Nevertheless, it is still possible to use their protective properties by copying the cottagers who liked to plant bushes around

*In southern England, however, rosemary is winter-hardy.

the vegetable patch with perennial herbs in between (see the chapter entitled 'Flowers, Shrubs and Roses'). This places a protective barrier around the vegetable patch. (For other uses, see the section on the preparation of liquid fertilizers.) When planted under rose trees, sage discourages aphides. It also keeps roses healthy (see the illustration facing page 105). Snails do not find it comfortable under any of these three herbs and tend to keep away from them. Besides being good for under-tree planting (and not only under roses), thyme is at home on walls.

Other, less decorative herbs are salad burnet, lemon balm and tarragon. Experience in the kitchen has shown that salad burnet (garden burnet) is a powerful detoxicant and is useful for making a 'clean sweep' of body poisons. It stimulates the root systems of other plants, which grow healthily in its vicinity.

Lemon balm always thrives in the garden and is an outstanding plant for bees. Hence it is always put in where bees will be needed to pollinate other flowers. Lemon balm has an enormous root system and it tends to spread itself, so it must be kept in control. It can then be prepared to make a liquid manure.

Tarragon, which should be found in every garden, is known to fortify the digestion. A sprig or two should always be put in the vinegar bottle or added to pickles. In the garden, it has a similar effect to the other herbs mentioned. Tarragon is very hard to raise from seed and it is best to ask the nurseryman for a slip to put in.

Rue is a little-known herb that is very decorative. It is a defence plant like those already mentioned, and is good to put around delicate shrubs or under roses.

Chives, a member of the onion family, is another herb that wards off pests and, in particular, all fungal diseases. It is very suitable for planting as a surround for rose trees. If it is not cut regularly, it will flower and is then ready for cutting and laying on the ground between strawberry plants, where its fungicidal action can take full effect. For winter use, remember not to add it to stews until it has been well frozen. It can be left where it has grown, but will freeze even better if the bulbs are taken up as fist-sized clumps and left lying in the open. If planted in pots, the chives will continue to grow inside for kitchen use. (Unless they have been subjected to frost, chives are likely to be attacked by aphides.) After use, the clump is put back outside and another one is brought into the house to provide leaves for clipping. In this way, a constant supply of leaf tips is on hand for kitchen use throughout the winter until the plants start growing out of doors again when the warmer weather comes.

Lovage and wormwood must also be mentioned. Although wormwood is really a wild flower, it is planted in the garden as a medicinal and pot herb, because it aids the digestion of heavy meals. Lovage and wormwood have a marked effect on pests in neighbouring plants but also tend to inhibit the growth of the latter. For this reason, they are best placed where they will decorate some out-of-the-way corner, ready for use in the kitchen at any time. The flowers of wormwood, not the leaves, are the parts used.

The above-mentioned perennial herbs add to the pleasure of the garden with their aromatic scents. They also attract bees, ward off pests, prevent plant diseases and are indispensable for the well-being of the garden.

Using Chopped Herbs

Are herbs still useful when they have to be cut? All herbs have to be cut down at times, even when they are in continuous use. They grow too big, they start to bloom, become unmanageable, give too much shade and, in short, need trimming. The first thing we can do with the trimmings is to turn them into a very valuable covering for vegetables of all sorts (e.g. chives placed around strawberries). When not applied directly, they can be used to prepare various types of compost, including chopped organic material. According to their properties, the chopped herbs are spread around the particular vegetables which need them.

We have already mentioned chives as a typical example. When placed between strawberries, this member of the onion family deters fungi. Other herbs can be laid underneath plants that attract large numbers of snails, e.g. the day-lily (*Hemerocallis*) or the larkspur. Again, they can be put down beside rows of lettuces – always on the surface compost, or on the small circular beds round shrubs.

The layer of herb cuttings will invariably protect the vegetables or flowers concerned. Of course, if there is a compost heap, this is the logical place for chopped herbs which will help the heap to rot down more quickly. There are, however, one or two herbs which should not form part of a compost heap, since they hinder not only plant growth but the rotting-down process as well. A good example of these is wormwood, the best place for which (if there are no rows of cabbages) is underneath the black currant bushes to ward off rust. The output is not particularly big, so that it is never difficult to find room for the cuttings under the bushes.

Plants as Fertilizers

There is no better fertilizer than a ferment made of any or all of the above-mentioned herbs, and in fact most gardeners have now heard of the liquid manure made from stinging-nettles. The fermentation of freshly cut herbs with added water is a natural process. The oft-asked question about how to make liquid plant manure, is answered by 'the fertilizer makes itself'. The containers used can be made of various materials although, naturally, wood or earthenware would be best. It would be pointless to measure out the water and piles of herbs in pints and pounds; usually the vessel is half filled with herbs and then topped up with water. Rainwater is best, of course, but, failing that, tap water will do.

Another question that is often asked is how long the liquid has to stand before it is 'ready'. The fermentation is a slow temperature-dependent process, which undergoes visible changes. Initially, the liquid turns cloudy and starts to become coloured until, in the end, it is a dark extract in which all the vegetable matter has disappeared. The fluid emits a smell, weak at first but eventually quite strong; if this is a nuisance, a few handfuls of rock powder may be stirred in. However, stinging-nettle brew will emit a smell only when disturbed by being stirred or poured out.

The use of the liquid depends on its degree of fermentation. In the early stages, it is especially suitable for preparing seedlings for planting out. Their roots are dipped in the fluid contained in a shallow vessel. Young plants which have been given this fertilizer are well on their way to healthy growth and development. Celery rust is inhibited by it for instance.

At this early stage, the brew may be sprinkled over foliage, say over an aphis-infested rose-bush or over a bush where it is thought, from past experience, that an attack of greenfly or mildew is likely to occur. When it has matured, the fertilizer may still be used as above if mixed half-and-half with water. The benefits of the treatment are quickly apparent. With fermentation well advanced a proper manure results, which will feed the plants and make good many soil deficiencies.

Other herbs may effectively be added to the basic nettle brew – as, for example, comfrey, a wild flower that doubles as a garden plant. The leaves of any member of the cabbage family are usable too and the cabbage ought to be regarded as more than something for the plate! In former times, it was prized as a medicinal plant and is still one of our most valuable vegetables, being full of healing power (see the chapter on page 91). The addition of cabbages or thinned out cabbage plants to the preparation will do much to make crops thrive.

Application

When is the best time to fertilize a garden that is being cultivated along correct biological lines? And what should be used for the job? It is always right to bring out the stinging-nettle liquid just described when we are tilling the soil, i.e. as a preliminary manure. The rule always holds good that plants ought never to be manured direct; it is the ground in which they are going to be put that has to be manured. This rule applies to manuring with specially fermented liquid just as much as to any other kind of manuring.

These natural brews return to the soil, and indirectly to the plants, what was originally taken out of the soil and could never be replaced in such well-balanced amounts by artificial fertilizers. These liquid manures made of stinging-nettles or of nettles mixed with other herbs, with all their health-giving ingredients, should first and foremost be used on the rows in which fruit-bearing vegetables are going to be planted.

Where the companion-planted garden is well arranged, the rows remain fixed from spring onwards and no further special treatment is required. The home-made liquid may also be used for strawberries for instance, at a time when the coming harvest is programmed, (i.e. in autumn when the next year's buds begin to form). The liquids are also used on trees, roses and shrubs when they start to sprout and then again when they are in full bloom, that is to say when their uptake from the soil is greatest. This is by way of pre-manuring for the following year. Ground that has been prepared with the organic fertilizers described here may be expected to support a luxuriant growth of healthy plants.

Other Liquid Fertilizers

There is no need to be too meticulous in making up these liquid fertilizers so long as care is taken not to include any growth-inhibiting herbs. Wormwood, parsley, mugwort and lovage have a special value for the garden, as we have already seen when considering their defensive powers. There is nothing wrong with making them into liquid fertilizer so long as it is kept separate for special use. These individual fertilizers are applied direct and *only* where there are specific problems such as fungal diseases, leaf curl and other unpleasant phenomena. Other special brews can be made from rhubarb leaves or horse-radish leaves. Either alone or mixed, these will do much to protect cabbages from club root.

When the stinging-nettle liquid is old, thick and concentrated, with a very strong smell, it can still (and there is no need to dilute it for this purpose) be

---

Example of a Well Covered Companion-planted Garden
Cabbage with celery
Lettuce with chervil and radish
Cucumbers with dill and basil.
All the 50 cm-wide spaces between the rows are covered with stinging-nettles, chopped herbs, grass, alternated for preference, when available, with chopped garden herbs, vegetable trimming and wild flowers. If woody material is chopped in as well, weeds will be discouraged. Rain and dew do their work as usual. If necessary,watering should be carried out on the compost alone, which acts as a filter and retains the moisture; however, the plants should only be watered when first planted.

poured round the roots of our trees, preferably at the beginning of winter. This concentrated nettle and herb mixture, with added chalk, is also used to treat tree trunks. It is painted on the bark with, if necessary, a little water-glass as an adhesive. Damage that is slow to heal in old trees can be cured in this way. For example, stinging-nettle liquid can be sprayed on where damage has been caused by frost. This is one more example of what a splendid help such fermented fertilizers are.

Finally, whenever such liquid fertilizers are used, a solid residue remains in the containers. A layer of this residue may be spread, in the course of the year, over one or more rows of plants – if there is any left over – and on sheet compost as well. If compost heaps are used, the residue will act as a good starter, just as it

---

Mustard and Field Beans are Used to Ensure the Health of Other Plants

Top left:
The mustard is cut when the next crop is due to follow. It will not disturb anything that is sown later (see the illustration facing page 16). The generous root system is left behind in the soil, while the leaves lie on top as a covering.

Top right:
This sample shows how quickly and luxuriantly mustard grows and how well its roots penetrate the ground. Soil that has been broken up like this is ideal for vegetables waiting to be planted out.

Centre left:
This picture of the root of the bean shows and explains why it is so beneficial as a preliminary crop. The nitrogen nodules seen here will release their goodness as a natural fertilizer for other plants. When the beans are 15–30cm high they are cut down and left lying as additional top compost.

Centre right:
A look beneath the layer of sheet compost reveals plenty of earthworm activity, showing the great value of this type of covering.

Below left:
Single digging in spring turns up a dark, humus-rich soil. This has been kept covered with sheet compost for some years.

Below right:
The same soil without composting. The picture was taken after heavy rain had been followed by heat.

does with sheet compost: because of the large quantity of nettles, rotting down occurs much more quickly.

**Companion Planting –
Set out in Diagrammatic Form**
It will be useful to conclude this set of chapters with a diagrammatic illustration:

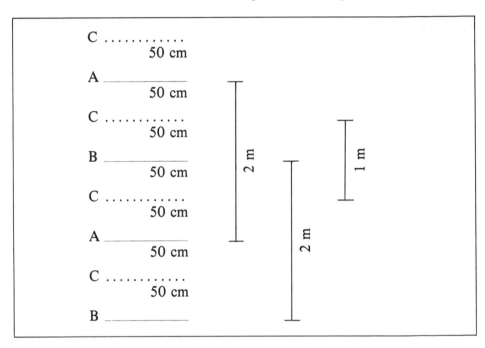

A Rows
RED, 2 metres apart; earmarked from May until the end of the vegetation period for tall or spreading crops. In early spring they are sown with a frost-resistant preparatory crop (mustard, field beans).
B Rows
GREEN, also 2 metres apart; yield two full crops in the first and second halves of the vegetation year.
C Rows
BLUE, 1 metre apart, making twice as many rows as the A or B rows; are reserved for species with a short vegetation time and compact growth.
(A list of the various species to be put in rows A, B and C has been given on page 30).

5.

Garden Animals
and Insects

When the gardener comes across any of the fauna living in his garden, he tends
to see them – and usually with some justification – as pests. Such creatures
range from greenfly, ants, snails, spiders, numerous caterpillars, woodlice,
earwigs and millepedes to moles, voles and the like.

If the gardener who is a conservationist avoids the use of poisonous
substances as a means of pest control, because he knows that the garden is a
home for useful creatures as well as for noxious ones, he should also take pains
to consider which species should be regarded as useful. The big question then is
which creatures should be allowed to survive and which should not? Perhaps we
ought to follow the example of nature and refrain from a policy of extermination.
All animals help to make up the cycle of existence, all have some significance
through their activities, their coming and their passing away. Each animal has
an effect on some other animal and is useful to the extent that it preserves the
balance of nature by keeping that other one in check. The perceptive gardener
can see a vital interplay in these happenings.

In previous chapters, I have dealt with the mutual relationships between
plants and between plants and soil. It will now be especially interesting and
instructive to think about the relationships between 'animals', plants and soil.

The arrival in the garden of particularly troublesome creatures, such as wire-
worm and cutworm, is exceptional. Their appearance should be regarded as a
clear sign of a soil that has become unsettled or has not yet achieved a balance.
(An example of this is when a meadow is ploughed up). The gardener needs to
proceed systematically against these obvious pests. When the soil is in order
again they will no longer be a problem. All other garden creatures can safely be
left to develop in a natural way; and I will explain how, within the community of

living things, the various animals 'keep one another in check', so that it is an over-simplification to talk about this or that species being 'harmful'. All must be present for the benefit of others which feed on them, and so that the useful animals have tolerable living conditions. Even when the presence of certain creatures indicates a disturbed balance, it is still possible to have a living, healthy garden.

So which animals are present in the garden? What tasks are they performing for the soil and for the plants? When are they useful and when do they become pests?

Microfauna

Most of the species occupying our gardens are invisible to us. They live in the ground and make their presence felt only in so far as the soil becomes more vital, more humic and thus more easy to work as its inhabitants are nourished by the addition of organic materials. In these conditions they multiply and support everything we do to promote humus forming.

These microscopic creatures are the most important component of the soil, and where they are deficient the fact is obvious because the soil is no longer in a proper state for tillage. Such a soil is hard to work and has to be helped with organic fertilizers of animal origin. With the provision of vegetable matter through surface compost, the life of the soil recovers. In other words, what has to be added is what nature itself would supply. Animals of various sizes live in the garden soil, deposit their excreta there, die there and manure it with their decomposing bodies. They live on their earthy environment, on rotting plant materials and on the multitudes of soil bacteria.

In addition to the microscopic animal world (the microfauna of the soil), there is the microscopic vegetable world (the microflora), which, in a similar way, is necessary for its tilth.

Larger Fauna

Garden fauna which is visible to the naked eye – but not as big as the hedgehog, squirrel, dormouse or sparrow, say – has its chief representative in the earthworm. Its activities and its tremendous value to the garden are well known. However, it thrives only in living soil where there is plenty of food for it. When present, it loosens the soil particles to allow free circulation of air and water. Thus the earthworm creates suitable living conditions for other organisms. What is more, it thoroughly mixes the soil and enriches it around the walls of its burrows. Needless to say, the earthworm can be harmed by saliferous fertilizer materials, and anyone who takes up biological gardening should avoid their use.

Molehills are occasionally encountered, as the visible and disturbing sign of the presence of moles, usually on untilled land such as meadows but rarely in the middle of a vegetable patch. Moles feel at home with a roof of grass over their heads and in unworked ground where they help to ventilate the soil. They also improve the soil and the earth they throw up is particularly fine and suitable for seed-boxes. If their mounds were not so unsightly, they would be welcome as predators preying on small rodents, including the voles which often share their runs. They also hunt for the white worm and cutworm which have multiplied so alarmingly since the beginning of the seventies. Finally, the mole enjoys a meal of snails and wire-worms.

Mole-crickets are another pest. They are found usually on withered plants. Wine-growing regions are their favourite haunts, especially where continuous monoculture of fastidious plants, which yield well only after excessive direct manuring, has upset the balance of the soil. Mole-crickets devour everything – including grubs, wire-worms and caterpillars – but mainly roots and plants; hence they are feared pests, and do good to a limited extent only.

The mole-cricket's natural enemies are starlings, blackbirds and shrews, all three being commonly found in most gardens. The mole-cricket also has the mole as its enemy, which is how it got its name. Once more, we see how closely interconnected the various factors are, because when the balance of the soil is restored, the pronounced destructive character of the mole-cricket alters.

Snails can hardly be regarded as anything but pests in the garden, and small slugs are even more destructive. These creatures can do a great deal of damage almost unnoticed. The problem of exterminating snails and slugs or keeping them under reasonable control is still being debated, (see the end of the chapter for further information on this). Yet even snails have their place in the biological scheme of things. Many species expel other types of snail, and the struggle between them may often be observed on the garden path. The grey slug (*Arion*) is notorious as an omniverous creature which will even devour weak and dying individuals of its own species. It is nature's 'waste-disposal man'. Snails, too, will keep one another in check.

Fortunately, snails do not attack all species of plants since they are to be found only on those plants which have no defence mechanism: plants which have just been planted out before they are well rooted and plants whose season is over and have become flaccid. They avoid plants with stinging hairs such as the stinging-nettle, borage and older cucumber plants. Young zinnia and larkspur, on the other hand, are examples of the sort of tender plant on which snails really like to feed.

Snails vex the gardener in a variety of ways, but are also necessary as food for many other creatures with all kinds of tasks to perform in the course of the gardening year and in the rhythm of nature. They form part of the diet of many birds which the gardener welcomes since they can help in the garden in other ways. These include the blackbird, the starling and the thrush. The hedgehog relishes snails; crows, moles and toads are fond of them too. Surprisingly enough, however, it is known that even some tiny flying insects, such as the glow-worm, kill snails, injecting their poisonous fluid into the snail's body. The snails that perish usually supply an unrecognized but considerable amount of nitrogenous manure to the place where they lived; some, however, are picked up by birds who fly away with them and eat them elsewhere – and, in this way, one thing lives on another.

The ground beetle is a fairly conspicuous insect. It lives not only on slugs and snails, but eats a large number of insect larvae. Caterpillars, too, go to make up its diet and it is used against woodland pests.

Earwigs are another familiar sight. They destroy aphides and shield lice and are particularly useful in orchards. However, they can become destructive when their animal prey is lacking and when they are thirsty; in these circumstances they switch over to plant food. Here and in many other instances, there is not much the gardener can do, because these variations are connected with seasonal variations in the weather. Whether the seasons are late or early makes a considerable difference. It is entirely possible for all these different creatures to be living in a garden without harm to plant growth, but if the previous year's weather was bad, some animals are favoured at the expense of others. This is the source of most of the problems during the rest of the year.

The Composition of the Animal Community
If extreme measures of pest control practically wipe out the green fly population in one year so that the ladybirds for example do not get enough to eat and so fail to multiply, it is to be expected that the following year will be a very good year for aphides. The ladybird has been chosen as an example because it is known to be so useful, especially for keeping aphides in check. To put it in a nutshell: a good year for pests means plenty of food for their natural enemies and an abundance of the latter in the following year! The picture opposite page 48 shows aphides and ladybirds together on the same branch. The green fly had appeared overnight but the ladybirds destroyed them, the net result being that the plant remained undamaged. What would have happened if one of the usual pesticides had been sprayed on the aphides? Without doubt, the helpful ladybirds would have suffered as well.

Interdependence
The question of the community of interests represented by animals, plants and soil deserves some mention. In practice this means that we must try to think in

terms of relationships, knowing that in the garden, just as in nature as a whole, all living things are interdependent. In the garden the following relationships should be observed:

Plants need other plants as partners in many different connections – see the sections on companion planting.

Cultivated plants need various herbs to accompany them; that is to say they need medicinal and pot herbs to promote their health and growth, to give shade and to protect them from pests and diseases.

Cultivated plants need wild flowers, which should be allowed to transmit their particular virtues until they start to get in the way and have to be removed. This subsidiary flora is often indispensable, as a protective covering for the soil and as a soil indicator.

Animals in the garden need plants; bees for example must be able to feed themselves and to collect nectar for their honey.

Plants need 'animals'; once again, the example of the bees comes to mind. Many flowers require bees and other insects to pollinate them before they can bear fruit.

Birds need plants to supply them with food, and they are also necessary as breeding places. These and other creatures (wasps for example) need protein-rich food for their young and so, incidentally, they help the gardener by picking up small insects which would, if left behind, turn into pests.

'Animals' in the garden need other 'animals' as regulators. A classical example of this is the one of the ladybird and the aphis, already mentioned. Take another look at the photograph of the infested rose bush. It may be seen from this familiar and enlightening example, that the ladybird, in feeding, reduces the aphis population but that sufficient aphides have to be present at a given time to ensure the survival of the ladybird.

'Animals' need wild flowers, on which to lay their eggs and rear their progeny. However, the beautiful butterflies, which are no longer able to find stinging-nettles or other wild flowers in most pitifully empty gardens, have no chance of reproducing themselves there any more; this is why we no longer see them sunning themselves or fluttering along the borders. The ladybird, too, requires the stinging-nettle as a breeding place.

The soil, which is the basis of all gardening activities, can achieve its prime condition only when it is integrated in the cycle of the building up and breaking down of organic materials. The decomposition products must remain available for the synthesis of new tissues. One way of bringing this about is through the microbial and other activity in surface compost. Only by this living give-and-take between the annual constructive and destructive forces of nature can a soil be created in which high-quality food plants grow.

When Animals and Insects become Pests

Snails are among the animals which easily become plagues. This is especially likely to happen when, owing to unusual weather conditions or to a disruption of the ordinary rhythm of the seasons, they are one-sidedly favoured. Clear indications were given at the start of this chapter concerning the effects different animals and plants living in the garden have on one another. Generally speaking, they hold one another in check, but there are occasions when one species (in this case the snail), manages to tip the balance of nature to its own advantage and starts to 'go on the rampage' as it were. The point is, what can be done about it?

The slug pellets so often used, even in a biologically cultivated garden, are poisonous and more harmful than is commonly assumed. Of course, they do not harm the plants, since the pellets are used in such a way that they do not form part of their nourishment; however these pellets are a danger to small children, and the dead or dying snails which have been poisoned are a hazard not only to the hedgehog but to other small animals attracted by an easy meal.

Birds, especially the insectivorous ones, including some favourite song birds which feed their fledglings on worms and small snails, are specially at risk. Even where the pellets are put down with care, dead birds are found in the neighbourhood, not excepting the garden itself. The snail's natural enemies suffer along with the snails.

If, in spite of all advice to the contrary, the reader is determined to use slug pellets, a great number of slugs and snails will be drawn to the places where the pellets have been strewn and there they will die. Immediate action must then be taken to pour lime or rock powder over the carcases to prevent animals and birds from eating them. What I would recommend is to gather as many slugs and snails as possible, morning and evening, and tip them into a pail of boiling water. This is more humane than leaving them to suffer a lingering death from slug pellets, and the number of snails is quickly reduced. This brew of snails and slugs can be poured over compost to enrich it. However, it should also be kept to ward off any anticipated invasion of snails. The pail is left standing for a few days until its contents start to smell strongly, and the brew is then poured around the endangered crops through the rose of a watering can at a suitable interval before harvesting. The spout of the can may be swung in wide arcs during pouring, because the liquid will work well even when thinly spread. However, sprinkling may also be done between rows or around a whole area. For example, strawberry beds may be treated in this way to keep them free from snails.

The same is true of a vegetable patch. The dead bodies of the snails are also used, laid between the rows or tipped out of the can as desired. The deterrent effect persists for several weeks and, what is more, the dead snails make a good fertilizer. Even in 1978 when there was a plague of snails, we succeeded in keeping our strawberry beds and vegetable rows entirely free from the pests. Elsewhere in the garden, underneath the bushes, there were snails in plenty, so it was possible to collect them to keep making fresh brews throughout the summer for liberal application around the places in need of protection. It was discovered that slug pellets, although they were an irresistable lure to large numbers of slugs and snails, were by no means as effective as the snail brew. The best of it was that the superior method did not cost a penny! The brew does not harm any of the plants on which it might accidentally fall. However, the gardener must guard against touching decaying slugs or snails with the bare hands, since this might have an adverse effect on small wounds.

Amateur gardeners usually worry over the presence of a few greenfly, but it must be remembered that a garden with no greenfly is a sterile garden. If there are no aphides there is nothing for the ladybirds to eat. Because aphides are so prolific, they are likely to make a come-back in the following year, but there will be no ladybirds to counter them. If greenfly really threaten to become a pest, a fairly strong but innocuous remedy can be made up: a half-and-half mixture of methylated spirit and water. This can be sprayed on by means of one of the syringes on the market. In the chapter entitled Flowers, Shrubs and Roses, the question is raised whether flowers are useful as a defence against pests, and suggestions are given on how they may be used in pest control.

Ants are almost always regarded as pests, as witness the many well known tips for exterminating them. The biologically orientated gardener is bound to wonder why and on what basis all types of ant are treated as pests, since there is no doubt about the only type that can be harmful. This is the small ant that milks aphides of their honey dew and stimulates them to keep eating. This, the only harmful ant, actually assists the aphides to attack plants unless certain herbs are put in nearby to discourage them. The herbs concerned have already been mentioned in another connection; they are lavender, sage and hyssop. Ants may also be repelled with a liquid preparation of ferns. This is poured on the small circular beds at the base of rose trees etc. and, in special cases, even over the infested plants themselves.

A great deal of damage may also be done by ants to strawberry beds. They tend to lift the plants out of the soil so that they wither. If wormwood is growing in the garden, it should be made into a hot brew and poured undiluted over the strawberry plants on alternate days when cold. All other species of ants are very useful in the garden. They ventilate the soil, crumble it and deacidify it. They are all humus-makers. There is no doubt that growth in general is better and more luxuriant where ants have their nest. Gardens, especially old gardens with wild corners where the hoe has not passed, often owe to the ants an exuberant show of spring flowers in positions where no seeds or bulbs have been put in by human hand. This is because ants are splendidly efficient planters, especially when it comes to spring flowers such as crocuses, snowdrops and lungwort (*Verbascum thapsus*), not to mention the many varieties of wild flowers with small seeds which are already resident in the garden – for example, purslane (*Portulaca*) and comfrey.

Later in the year, ants help the peony to exhibit the fairest and most perfect blooms as they run about on its unopened buds. This is really something worth watching each season! The ants scurry along the fine veins on the buds, which exude a sap they love. They continue this activity until the flower opens, when their task is fulfilled. No harm is ever done to any of these peony blossoms. Without the constant activity of such 'squads' of ants, the rose chafer's depredations would be considerable. What has been observed on the peony has been seen repeated quite remarkably in other multiflorous plants.

Other Animal Pests

The main thing for the organically-minded gardener to remember is that there is no need to fear that a disaster is bound to occur sooner or later. He knows the dependence of one creature on another and the natural cycles through which they run in the course of a year, he knows the effects on them of climate and weather, and he can set to work accordingly.

In the chapter dealing with weeds in the garden, many examples are given of how certain plants can serve as a defence against animal pests. It will be recalled that stinging-nettle liquid compounded with the juices of wild flowers can do much to help. The undiluted fluid is poured around the roots or on the circular beds underneath trees and standard roses. Its protective effect is absolutely astonishing. Often it is sufficient to spray the liquid (or the corresponding infusion) or to loosen the soil around the roots and water.

6.
Growing Fruit

What has already been said about cultivating the flower garden and the vegetable patch does not complete the story, and a brief mention must be made of fruit growing. Plenty of advice is available in literature on the subject of growing berries and stone-fruit, but there is a pressing need to consider the biological methods of cultivation.

The present-day practice of monoculture in all areas of horticulture including soft fruit and orchard fruit has greatly aggravated the problems of disease and infestation. While commercial orchards remain a law unto themselves in the matter, it is common sense for the owner of an allotment or domestic garden to observe the same rules as he applies to the other parts of his garden. Quite often, quick benefits are sought by abandoning the usual chemical preparations for so-called biological ones. However, this is not enough in itself.

It is necessary to set to work from ecological as well as biological points of view, and to take into account the needs of plants, their natural habitats and what types of soil and climate are suited to them. Points to notice are the condition of the soil, the lie of the land and the microclimate of the garden. Trees and bushes should be accommodated to suit the life of the neighbouring vegetation. What is more, the same rule applies that prevention is better than cure and that efforts should be made to discover and eradicate the causes of disease and other problems.

Soft Fruit
All soft fruit, especially strawberries and raspberries, were originally woodland plants which feel at home in glades or on the outskirts of woods. That is where they enjoy shade, a constantly covered soil and an ecological environment

which suit them best. Woods also contain the wild varieties of currant and gooseberry, and the conditions in which these thrive can, if studied, give useful information about their requirements. To provide the cultivated varieties with comparable conditions, their plots should be chosen with care, and circumstances arranged so that the berries will remain healthy and grow prolifically – even in a back garden. Since they become a permanent feature in the garden, bushes are easiest to manage in this respect.

In the last chapter, mention was made of old cottage gardens where, it is worth adding, raspberry canes etc. would be interspersed with other shrubs, bushes and small trees. They displayed the sort of companion planting that might well serve as a pattern for our modern gardens. By and large, the kind of damage universally deplored in our own day and age could be avoided if we abandoned the practice of monoculture and put in other species to break up the monotonous rows of identical bushes.

Positioning the Bushes, Manuring and Tilling the Soil

An airy position with some shade is essential. Berry bushes fare badly in waterlogged soil or when they are too enclosed, and it is not good for them to be planted against the side of a house or, conversely, in a very sunny location.

Stinging-nettle liquid makes an excellent fertilizer for all soft fruit. It should be applied undiluted, except when it seems too thick, in which case it is thinned half-and-half with water. The best times for application are, first, when the young leaves begin to sprout and, second, when the berries have been gathered. For long-term manuring, mulch with shredded organic material as described on pages 41–43.

Liquid or solid animal manure straight from the stable or cowshed should not be used where soft fruit is being grown, for fear of adverse reactions. Much harm has been done to berry bushes by such ill-considered dunging; in some cases, the plants have shed their leaves prematurely and cast their fruit.

The soil under gooseberries and currants must always be covered. Shredded organic manure should be used but, in contrast to that used for the vegetable patch, straw is the best ingredient. This straw mulch, which is recommended only for perennials, is piled deep so as to come up to the branches of the bushes. In the course of the year it becomes compacted and is renewed in autumn without anything being done to disturb the soil. The deep litter deprives perennial weeds (such as bindweed) of light, and gets rid of them. Eventually the straw rots down to give a dark, humic soil.

In the first year of this form of berry growing, the soil should be inspected in autumn to see if it is loose enough. If it has become hard for any reason, it will have to be loosened as described in the section on vegetables: the ground is prodded with a fork without being turned over and is then recovered.

When gooseberries are blemished with mildew, which is quite likely if new growth is not pruned, spraying with an infusion of horsetail will help. If the bushes have been planted in a suitable (i.e. airy) place, and if they are pruned in spring, mildew will no longer occur.

Companion Plants for Soft Fruit

Tansy is useful for mixing with all berry bushes in order to keep them healthy. If the bushes are attacked by rust, an underplanting of wormwood will help in the proportion of one wormwood plant to every two or three currant bushes – that is, the former are put in the spaces between the latter.

The 'accompanying flora' in the woods is the plant community in which such plants grow wild. Obviously, they need something similar when under cultivation. The medicinal herbs already present in the garden are best for this purpose (although the straw should not cover these helper plants).

To discourage mice, which incidentally we have never seen here in forty years after adopting the right methods of cultivation, plants which mice dislike may be put in (see the section on warding off mice by companion planting); and the elderberry liquid should frequently be poured underneath the bushes. Anything growing in the rest of the garden (weeds, old tree stumps, vegetable refuse) may beneficially be used for these bushes. It does not matter in what form they are prepared – whether as liquid manure or compost, whether as a mulch or as some other form of fertilizer.

Note: pruning berry bushes is simple – the oldest shoots (which appear overgrown) are simply cut out to make room for the younger shoots which will produce the best yield.

Raspberries

The raspberry, which with the bilberry or whortleberry is the best known of the berries adopted for domestic use, is very sensitive to any sort of quick-acting nitrogenous material. Raspberry canes should be grown as naturally as possible and special care must be taken to avoid fresh animal manure! For one thing, the smell attracts undesirable insects, whereas the main aim is to produce fruit which will be free from maggots.

Quite apart from this, raspberries should be grown in a soil with a suitable covering of straw plus a certain amount of wilted leaves. This can be laid on in autumn. Then, before a fresh covering is applied for spring, it is an excellent idea to apply a compost fertilizer. It is equally advantageous to put chopped organic material mixed with rock powder round the raspberries; this will decompose and form a sound fertilizer. Liquid manure – by which is meant thinned plant liquids, preferably those made from elderberry, tansy and horsetail – is given in the same way as to other perennials: at the time of sprouting and when the canes are being tidied up and pruned. Nothing could be simpler for getting everything in readiness for the coming year.

For the finishing touch, marigolds, which have been prized from antiquity as a healing herb, can be sown among the raspberries. Its roots benefit the soil and the raspberry canes can develop without becoming diseased.

Currants

The black currant thrives without trouble if the same measures are taken as described above. The plant looks after itself in that it avails itself of everything it can reach with its roots. Therefore the bushes should be fairly well spaced. They are not the best of neighbours for weak plants. It does not generally suffer from pests* – its leaves have a powerful preservative action and can be employed in making pickles (gherkins, for example). Rust, however, does attack the backs of black currant leaves, but this may be countered by growing wormwood in the vicinity.

Complaints are often made about early leaf-fall in black currants. This may be prevented by watering well with stinging-nettle liquid at the beginning of the season. The solid residue left behind when the liquid is decanted is used to cover the ground round the base of the bushes.

Strawberries

Strawberries bring real problems into the garden. These are due to the fact that the plant has been removed so far from its woodland habitat that it has become sensitive and fastidious. It is a shallow-rooted plant and yet on empty, open land, so subject to variations of wet and dry, it is expected to grow and flourish – usually under the relentless glare of the sun. In these conditions, the strawberry plant is unable to survive without some help.

Even when they are young plants, strawberries should never be isolated or planted in bare, open soil. Here, they would have to withstand all the influences of the weather without any protection and before being properly rooted. There is great danger that the soil will become compacted if, after every rainstorm it is dried out by the sun. What is more, every pest has free access and notable damage is done unless the problem is tackled early on. Therefore, it is not only advisable but necessary to integrate the young plants in the companion planting system, that is to say to plant them in open rows pre-sown with some herb such as mustard. When this is done, the young strawberries have a protective plant

*However, black currant bushes can suffer from 'big bud'.

near them as well as shade overhead, and they are then sturdy enough to survive the winter. Experience has taught us to use rows previously occupied by some variety of vegetable that supplies nitrogen to the soil – the pea, say – and also to sow mustard. The strawberries should also be planted at reasonable intervals. Another way is to plant the strawberries in rows where some other crop is already established, with endives for instance. The endives are used in the course of autumn and winter and the strawberries, which have grown under their protection, are then left with the rows to themselves.

Whether they are put in with mustard or in some row where a salad plant is already growing, strawberries should be given some leeks or onions as neighbours – see the sections on early sowing on page 17 and onion growing on page 25. Stinging-nettle, comfrey or cabbage liquids are used as already described, either by themselves or mixed (a mixture is particularly beneficial to strawberries).

In early winter, it is important to do some advance manuring for the coming year after the newly planted strawberries are well rooted (and also in permanent beds). Stinging-nettle liquid is poured near the plants. It is equally important to spread shredded organic material around and between the plants. The species of which this chopped compost is made should be those which grow in woodland or some similar soil; for example, use spruce and fir twigs, or pieces of juniper and fern or thin twigs from undergrowth. When foliage is available, it should be rotted down separately and turned several times so that it does not clump together. It can then be mixed in under the covering material, as for raspberries. Rock powder should be sprinkled over the whole preparation and no further nutrients are required in spring; simply supply a covering of mulch composed of heterogeneous materials. However, some watering is necessary, with an infusion of valerian say, to encourage the formation of flowers and fruit.

Since strawberries are primarily for eating raw, it ought to be possible to pick and eat them without washing them. Therefore, before they are gathered, the paths between the rows are covered with straw to stop rain spattering mud on the fruit. If the gardener observes these few rules, he will be rewarded with a crop of healthy, luscious berries. Mould will not be much of a problem, particularly if onion liquid is added to the plant fertilizer used in autumn. (For details on the value of the onion as a protection against fungal diseases, see the section on Flowers, Shrubs and Roses.) Note, too, that it is advisable to plant strawberries of more than one variety as mutual pollinators.

In the cultivation of strawberries, it has proved useful to mow off the leaves after the berries have been picked and to let them dry under the hot sun for burning. This is a hygienic measure. However, in a wet season, the leaves are added to compost, which will cope with anything, even with slightly mouldy material. The plants will start sprouting again surprisingly quickly and it will be necessary to thin them out.

The additional plants for the companion planting effect are put in (see the sections on onions and leeks), manure is spread and, if no suitable mulch is available, mustard can be sown. This freezes in winter to form the required compost. Distances between the rows will have to be decided by the gardener according to the land available. If a two-metre spacing (see the inside cover diagram) is chosen, that is to say if the strawberries are planted in two rows, two metres apart, from which peas have been cleared, this will leave a good mixed crop between the rows in the first year. Then, from the second year, when a path is needed (covered with straw) a middle row, one metre away, is available for another crop. The runners from the older plants will soon spread out and supply new plants without any added expense. All this should occur if the strawberries are provided with as close an approximation as possible to their natural woodland conditions, and are able to propagate by their usual mode of vegetative reproduction.

Now if it becomes desirable to renew the plants in the initial row when they are still in production but have begun to yield smaller fruit, we must let things work in reverse: the younger plants in the new row must be permitted to send out runners to replenish the old row after the old stock has been lifted and the soil has been brought back into good condition by composting and sowing with herbs. This supplies the answer to the ever-recurring question of how long strawberries should be left in. The time to remove them is when their leaves become discoloured, when the fruit is reduced in size and when no more runners are produced (which can be taken as a sure sign). However, the companion planting gardener has so much scope for variation that he has no need to wait until the last moment, but can renew his stock without trouble and expense in good time.

Fruit Trees in Flower

At the same time of year as fruit trees are flowering, the vegetable rows are clearly in evidence. The vegetables were put in as a so-called frost sowing. At least three weeks advantage over the spring crops is apparent. Anyone who wants a good crop of fruit from trees and bushes must treat the garden as a compact whole.

The bushes, summer flowers and herbs left growing round the perimeter of the enclosure attract hive bees and bumble-bees and so help the pollination of fruit and vegetables. An important part is played by spices which flower later in the year. These are planted in the free rows if they have not already been sown.

The hedge in the background is a reservation for animals and wild flowers which will play their part in the course of the gardening year.

This type of planting and care is applicable to larger layouts which are not really of the companion planting type. Here again, there must be no planting in bare, open soil but (perhaps after being cleared of an early crop of potatoes), the ground should be quickly sown with mustard, partly to discourage nematodes, and when this is no more than hand high the strawberries should be planted in it. Manuring and composting are carried out as previously described. Planting the strawberries in mustard protects them and provides them with the necessary microclimate.

Some thought has to be given to row spacing before planting. The least distance between rows should be one metre, to make room for walking between them later, but two metres is better as it allows for intermediate lines of other crops. For easy fruit picking the rows must not be placed too near one another.

Whether strawberry plants form an integral part of our consolidated companion planting system or are grown somewhat apart, a back-up of this form of gardening is necessary for them. The strawberry area may be kept completely healthy by providing some nectar-rich flowers nearby for the bees, by using the recommended plant liquids as preliminary fertilizers, by including medicinal herbs in our compost and by taking care to create a favourable microclimate in the early stages.

Tree Fruit

Trees are a well established feature of older gardens, and where such a garden is being laid out for the first time, the gardener should make a point of planting trees even if they are non-productive, so that they can throw a certain amount of shade. Woodland trees of widely varying shapes and sizes lend charm to the

---

Corners of the Vegetable Patch

Top:
Annuals form part of the vegetable crop. These are both medicinal and pot herbs. Here, dill is springing up among the cucumbers; basil is also coming up but it is not yet visible. Annuals make no demands on space and may be sown simultaneously with a wide variety of other crops. Besides being so welcome in the kitchen, they do a great deal for the garden. Since culinary requirements are great and the young leaves are preferred, herbs should be brought on continuously in different stages of growth. Both pictures illustrate this occurring in different patches.

Bottom:
A second row of cabbages may sometimes be sown as an exception to the rule if both rows are flanked by protective herbs and spices and the intermediate spaces are covered with medicinal herbs.

garden, in addition to forming a wind-break and a shelter from the heat of the sun. They create a beneficial microclimate and need scant attention. All the same, they are deserving of care and preservation, since song-birds nest in them and they are both home and a source of nourishment for many small creatures. Their presence promotes the life and well-being of a walled plot and turns it into an ecological unit.

Putting in New Fruit Trees

Our newly planted trees will need something to get them off to a good start. Usually a large planting hole is cut in the ground to receive them, and this should then be filled with fresh soil in healthy condition if the quality of the local soil is poor. In addition, it would do no harm to imitate the old countrymen, who would throw anything from a handful to a small pailful of prime barley grain in the hole to lie just below the roots. The quantity used depends on the size of the tree, that is to say on whether it is a standard size or of some low-bush or espalier variety. As the grain germinates beneath the roots, heat is generated and growth hormones are released. Since the barley is unable to shoot after germinating, it eventually rots away to provide still more nourishment for the roots. Nettle liquid is also applied, both before and after planting. The earth used to fill the hole may be mixed with compost.

When the planting is done in spring, the bed at the base of the tree should be undersown. Spinach is suitable for this purpose, since it germinates and grows quickly, is soon grown and, when its leaves and roots have rotted down after the former have been chopped off, it supplies plenty of nutrients to the soil. What is more, the undersown vegetation shades the ground and prevents it from drying out and hardening. If you wish to be sure of having trees with healthy-looking foliage unspotted by blight, trees which fruit at the right time and are not ravaged by pests, the treatment you give them should be based on the main principles of nature.

Soil Covering, Manuring, Care of the Trunk

The great number of growing things found in a companion-planted garden – vegetables, medicinal and culinary herbs, shrubs, bushes and wild flowers – is a condition of this natural treatment.

Older trees are treated along the same lines as the young ones. If the measures are to be carried out correctly, a sufficiently large circular bed around each tree is essential. During the winter, it has to be covered with half-rotted compost – especially with shredded organic material as described in the appropriate section. Animal manure (well rotted farmyard manure) and rock powder are mixed into the compost or mulch. This covering can be hand-high.

In spring the tree should be given a strong dose of manure in the form of comfrey and stinging-nettle liquid. Elder liquid should be kept available in case it is needed to discourage mice. Later on, the round bed at the base of the tree is sown with some herb such as nasturtium, mustard or spinach, or even with marigold or purslane. This will not be necessary if ground ivy is growing there already. It is a wild flower that not only provides the desired cover but is also really useful for improving the soil. These medicinal herbs, even though admittedly some of them can be classed as weeds, supply their healing substances, collect dew and discourage pests: and so the beds around the trees are kept healthy.

Hence manuring is performed with what is offered by the garden itself: with nettle liquid for nutrition, with onion liquid to prevent fungal attacks, with horse-tail (*Equisetum*) or tansy for health and with elder liquid to keep rodents away. All these plant liquids can be blended for use on fruit trees.

Such measures are preventive and supportive. If the liquids are applied twice a year, at the time of budding and when the crops have been picked, and if a covering of shredded organic material is also applied twice a year, the tree can hardly avoid remaining healthy. Success does, however, depend on mixing plants that fertilize, plants that heal and plants that protect when preparing the liquids and the various types of compost. When this is done, the riches of the garden are placed at the disposal of its trees.

In winter, extra attention should be paid to the trunk. A thick stinging-nettle liquid, stirred up with *Algomin* or *Preicobakt* (or an equivalent seaweed preparation*) plus a little water-glass, is painted all over the trunk up to the branches or as far as the hand can reach. This disinfects the bark, cleanses, heals and nourishes it.

Aphides

A word is now in order on the subject of aphides, since so many gardeners complain about their attacks on their trees. What is required is knowledge of the cause of the trouble and what can be done about it. The damage inflicted by aphides is often slight, although the insects themselves do look unsightly. Since aphides are always 'latent', or hiding away and not easily detectable, they are ready to spring into action, so to speak, whenever conditions are right. Thus the onset of sultry or dry weather and thus an uncertain water supply can trigger an attack. Even the gardener can encourage aphides by letting the ground dry out or harden, or by some similar procedure.

* Chase Organics are suppliers of liquid extracts of seaweed, and Organic Farm Supplies also stock seaweed preparations, among them *Alginor*

There is little that can be done about changes in the weather, droughts and so on, but the soil at the base of the trees can be prevented from drying out in the ordinary way by ventilating it, covering it and sowing it with some suitable seed (as described earlier) so that the soil is shaded overhead and well broken up by rootlets below. Manuring by fits and starts, especially with fresh unrotted animal manure and uneven watering which does not get down into the soil, are to be avoided. Also the trees should not be planted too close to one another. If necessary, they should be thinned out so that the air can circulate freely between them.   ,

Before thinking of spraying pesticides on the aphides, the following simple measures should be tried: the soil at the base of the trees can be broken up where it has crusted, so that the air can penetrate it. The best fork to use for the purpose is a two-tined fork, as it spares the roots. After it has been worked, the ground should be given a good soaking and not just a token sprinkling.

Better still, drench the earth with stinging-nettle liquid after it has been loosened. Spraying should be resorted to only when the aphides are persistent. In the domestic garden, an infusion of horsetail or wormwood will probably be adequate but, if something stronger is needed, a half-and-half mixture of water and methylated spirit will do the trick.

Plants that Attract Bees

A great deal of the success of an orchard is due to the rest of the garden – especially to the parts where flowers are growing. There will be plenty of honey-bees and bumble-bees to fertilize the blossom on the fruit trees if the flowers which attract them are out in bloom from early spring onwards. And it must not be forgotten that some of the wild flowers inhabiting our gardens are very attractive to bees.

Every free space in the garden can be sown with phacelia. This is a plant that will cover the soil, break it up with its root system and keep it shaded. This small, feathery plant is excellent at collecting dew; when it comes into bloom, swarms of bees are continually flying in and out of the blue flowers, so that their humming swells through the summer air.

It might be thought that this is all that is involved, but that would be a mistake. The nests of bumble-bees gradually increase in number because of the favourable conditions, and these insects make their homes in the garden and are ready to start work in it as soon as spring arrives. The gardener must do everything possible to ensure that the insects are ready to pollinate the flowers at the right time. He or she must never put down poison, even on paved paths – since most of the bumble-bee nests are under these. The garden should afford protection to the insects so that they in their turn can give it their service.

7.

Flowers, Shrubs
and Roses

Anyone laying out a garden on untilled soil will have some notion of what he hopes it will look like when finished. An ideal example would be one of the old cottage gardens still to be found in rural areas. The vegetable patch forms the main part, but flowers are planted round the borders. If there is insufficient room near the house, cabbages and beans will be cultivated in a nearby field around the edges of a root crop.

The traditional cottage garden is enclosed by a line of fruit bushes and ornamental shrubs, according to the cottager's fancy, together with a leafy tree or two. Bordering the bushes or the vegetable beds, as the case may be, are the herbs, which would never be absent from a countryman's domain. They are used as pot-herbs in the kitchen and also as veterinary remedies.

This model plan for gardens, which has proved its worth over so many hundreds of years, cannot always be copied, especially when we are dealing with a piece of land that has already been planted. There may be other reasons discouraging imitation: the situation of the ground say, or the individual preferences of the gardener. The latter may wish to do what the neighbours are doing, and go in, say, for lawns and rose beds.

Managing an Ornamental Garden Organically
The question we wish to consider here is whether it is possible, even in an ornamental garden, to do without the recommended poison sprays or, in other words, to maintain the health of various plants by careful mixed cultivation. It is immaterial whether or not the layout of the garden is in the form and style of some ideal example; what is important is to plant species which will be mutually supportive and protective – in exactly the same way as was suggested for the vegetable patch.

In the case of the vegetable garden, all biological problems are admittedly easier to solve, since humus production proceeds continuously, year in and year out. There is also the advantage of crop rotation, which of course is not possible in an ornamental garden. Therefore it is hardly surprising that, faced with aphis-infested roses and blighted irises, some so-called 'biological gardeners' should operate in two different ways: some refrain from spraying their vegetables and soft fruit, while using chemical treatments on their decorative plants with the excuse, 'We don't eat them; all we want to do is to look at them.' However, neither the gardener nor his unfortunate plants are benefited in the long run. The life of the soil and the environment generally are harmed, and the natural accompanying flora is more or less extirpated, quite apart from the fact that such measures also destroy the useful creatures which would soon have been hard at work eating up garden pests.

A further consequence of these harsh treatments is that what is grown is restricted to a few long-lived species. Thus a one-sidedness is introduced into the garden that is reflected in a limited microflora and microfauna. The soil then becomes deficient and this deficiency has a detrimental effect on the few varieties which are grown. In this way, special difficulties are often encountered in ornamental gardens; therefore, it is advisable to adopt the same mixed culture methods here as well.

The plants' basic requirements should always be respected when a garden is being newly planted or filled up. If the gardener cares for the land, he should be able to tell the difference between alkaline and acid soils and what their qualities are. This may also mean having to do without certain preferred specimens according to the suitability of the soil.

It is not always realized that roses, for instance, ought never to be planted next to a warm wall – however pretty they might look there – because woodland plants, of which the rose is one, does not take kindly to glaring sunshine, but enjoy light shade and an airy situation. They also prefer ventilated soil, as already mentioned, provided there is also some soil cover.

Undersowing and Underplanting

This soil cover can well be provided by the undersowing of spinach and mustard at the start of the gardening year. Phacelia is also particularly useful in this respect, since not only does it provide a low cover of elegant leaves but later on proves very attractive to bees with flowers which beautify the garden.

Plants such as pennycress (*Lysimachia mammularia*), violets and ground-ivy, which produce a mass of root fibres, are not suitable for undersowing or underplanting. Nasturtiums are best under roses. They inhibit the growth of weeds and keep the main plants healthy. A very good underplanting species which is, however, only suitable for shady places is the periwinkle, which has the added advantage of not becoming too firmly rooted.

If bishopsweed (*Aegopodium podagraria*), for example, has established itself among the irises, a properly prepared cover of shredded compost containing no weed seeds in itself will help to clear the soil progressively, so that the bishopsweed can be pulled out. Chopped compost also acts as a protection against frost, besides making a good fertilizer during the year. Other fertilizers have been discussed in the section on liquid manures, where you will find notes on how to avoid pests and diseases using these natural means.

Avoiding Monocultures

Cottage gardens, which have already served as an example of good layout, can also supply a few hints on what to plant. Flower beds, for instance, are never planted with a single species; there are no massed ranks of asters, begonias, pansies or dahlias. In most cases, some species are used as the leading plants and others act as helpful adjuncts; for even in a decorative setting, the gardener can ward off pests and diseases by suitable companion planting. All the flowers in the garden possess healing properties, whether it is in the blossom, leaf or root.

The same cannot very often be said of the florist's fancy blooms or of the new strains and hybrids being developed today. These so-called 'improvements', paraded as splendid specimens are in fact pathetic blown-up versions of original compact forms. Whatever improvement they may boast has been obtained at the expense of scent, lasting quality or resistance to disease, and often at the expense of vigour as well. Rose hips are an especially rich source of vitamins, but only if they are gathered from the wild rose or from one of the old roses containing precious scents and other vital principles which have remained unchanged for centuries; such roses include the cabbage roses (*Centifolia*), Damask roses, French roses (*Gallica*), Bourbon roses etc. Selection is very important here. It is not enough, where roses are concerned, to ask for a polyanthus or a floribunda or for some other type, since there is much variation within the main groups. The nurseryman's catalogue should be carefully read for details of colour and height and for plainly stated information about the plant's winter hardiness, susceptibility to mildew and so on.

Before going on to consider the question of companion planting in an ornamental garden, it is best to summarize the things which should be avoided in such a garden: planting in blocks, which really do nothing to add to the beauty of a garden but are spread out like a feast for the pests which prey on them; leaving beds of exposed soil, instead of covering them with shredded compost; mixing plants solely on the basis of their size and colour, without taking into consideration their active principles and their protective value for other plants; the suppression of certain 'weeds' which naturally accompany some of our garden flowers, helping them to resist pests or attract the bees, e.g. the harebell and many others. (These wild plants can be removed later in the year if they do become a nuisance.)

Companion Planting in Rose and Shrub Borders

The accompanying pictures should serve as examples of effective companion planting. The way in which the mixed cultivation of vegetables is managed can and should be imitated in the flower section. Cultivation of the soil with a view to promotion of healthy biological activity is a prerequisite for success here too.

If, in the course of time, roses or shrubs deteriorate or become more liable to attack by pests, this shows that further attention is needed. The first thing to try in such a case is to plant herbs around them, (see the chapter on the cultivation of medicinal and culinary herbs). All plants of the onion family, especially garlic, are highly beneficial to health. Garlic itself should be planted in autumn alongside all plants such as the rose which are subject to the ravages of mice. When planted around the outside of borders with sage, thyme, hyssop and lavender (and when these herbs are allowed to grow freely in the roses), garlic will certainly keep pests of all kinds at bay. Neither slugs nor snails will be found underneath these plants, and you will never see ants under or around lavender.

The various sorts of mallow should also find a place among the roses and flowering shrubs, including hibiscus which is made into a flower tea; bergamot and the true balm with its powerful scent, are also valuable plants in this section of the garden.

Perhaps first place among the protective plants should be given to the crown imperial (*Fritillaria*), well known for its ability to discourage mice and voles. It is loved by bees which visit it assiduously and the crown imperial is an especially good neighbour to lilies (tiger, Madonna, martagon, Turk's cap etc.), for which it can serve as a 'trap-plant'. Both in the woods and in the garden the lily beetle can become a very serious pest. It lays its eggs in the withering stalks of the *Fritillaria* and since use of chemical insecticides is out of the question, for the organic gardener, the pests must be removed by physically gathering the stalks together with the eggs and larvae and destroying them. If it is exploited in this way, the crown imperial will make a very good neighbour to other plants. A scattering of lilies and crown imperials in rose and shrub beds and borders is not only beautiful, therefore, but also useful. Lilies require shade at their feet and should be grown together; isolated specimens do not thrive. Because their requirements in respect of soil and position are so similar, it it sensible to plant these three together.

As already mentioned, garlic (one of the health-promoting members of the onion tribe) may usefully be planted among lilies. The latter are menaced by snails below ground and also by mice: both pests are discouraged by garlic. The pot marigold (*Calendula*) is another protective plant; it is easily grown from seed and needs little attention. The Latin name comes from the *Kalends*, the first day of the Roman month, and it will flower well throughout the year if cut at monthly intervals. Since its main virtue resides in its roots, it is important to have it growing next to other plants all the year round. When sown underneath roses and other bushes, it inhibits nematodes. The orange petals can be harvested for their medicinal value.

French marigold (*Tagetes*) is another medicinal herb suitable for companion planting. It has a well known nematode-inhibiting effect in the root region. However, it is the varieties with a strong, unpleasant odour that must be planted; the new, odourless varieties are hopelessly ineffective!

The four-lobed spurge (*Euphorbia lathyris*) is a really good-neighbour plant wherever voles are active. *A word of warning:* the milk that kills the animals which nibble at the plant also injures human mucous membranes, so be careful when planting spurge! Children must not be permitted to come into contact with it.

Wild chamomile (*Matricaria chamomilla*) is useful for planting wherever there are shrubs. Another good plant for the rose and shrub garden is mullein (*Verbascum*), a biennial, traditionally used in herbal medicine. Bees are always attracted to this plant and so it is much prized by bee-keepers. Borage (*Borago officinalis*) helps to break up the soil with its spreading roots. Its blue, star-shaped flowers are very pretty and are also full of medicinal virtues. Both mullein and borage combine usefulness with beauty when planted among other plants. Taking a hint from the old cottage or monastery gardens, or indeed from the model layouts of modern botanical gardens, it should be realized that the recent predilection for ornamental planting is just a fashion.

In old-fashioned gardens, lupins (*Lupinus*) are planted with peonies (*Paeonia*), monkshood (*Aconitum*), foxglove (*Digitalis*), elecampane (*Inula*), hound's tongue (*Cynoglossum*), campion (*Lychnis*), dame's violet (*Hesperis*), Michaelmas daisy (*Aster*), costmary (*Chrysanthemum balsamita*), iris (*Iris germanica*), day lily (*Hemerocallis*), stock (*Matthiola*), and many other small plants, including many annuals. In addition, marguerites (*Chrysanthemum*), larkspur (annual *Delphinium*), bell-flowers (*Campanula*), sunflowers (*Helianthus*), heliotropes, violets, bleeding heart (*Dicentra*) and lilies (especially *Lilium candidum*) were planted. All these were put in together – the shorter varieties alongside the vegetable patch, the taller species in the border running round the garden. The roses included the Damask and moss roses, both white and red. Box too was always present in such a garden.

Care was taken to include trees and shrubs which could be used in herbal medicine: elder (*Sambucus*), lilac (*Syringa*), honeysuckle (*Lonicera*) or hazel (*Corylus*). Certain forms of companion planting proved especially valuable. For example, the grape hyacinth was found to protect tulips from the ravages of mice. What is more, it was found to be wiser not to underplant roses with mice-attracting tulips but with narcissi (*Narcissus*) as these are not subject to damage by pests. Vegetable patches are often interplanted with perennial herbs together with St John's wort (*Hypericum*), valerian, and tansy, but these will also fit well into an existing flower bed.

Medicinal herbs may be employed as fertilizer material and to ward off pests here as recommended for the vegetable garden. Particular attention should be paid to what has already been said about the protective power of medicinal herbs and wild flowers and about their use in the preparation of liquid manures etc.

When the Garden has Become 'Too Big'

Since a garden ought to be no larger than the human strength available for cultivating it, a time will come sooner or later when it becomes too big to manage. When this happens, part of it can be given over to suitable plants which are pleasing to the eye but require no attention, thus reducing the area under active cultivation. Especially suitable for this purpose are the various *Lamium* species, for example, the yellow dead-nettle (*Lamium galeobdolon*), which enjoy the leaf-fall from overhanging trees and bushes. In the flowering season, the yellow dead-nettle, or archangel as it is also called, bears splendid yellow 'candles'.

A garden planted according to the companion planting system may look rather out of the ordinary, it is true, but its spaciousness and balance encourage relaxation and improve health. Such a garden will lead to continual new observations and conclusions and will increase awareness of the inter-connectedness of all the processes going on in Nature.

8.
The Garden
and Nutrition

Whereas, as mentioned in the Introduction, it was practical problems entailed in feeding people and animals belonging to a rather large household that gave the initial impetus for biological gardening, experience has shown that this new type of cultivation can provide some keys to health.

The question is often asked whether it is worth while to put so much thought and effort into the cultivation of vegetables. No one would deny the sense of helping the domestic budget by growing a large part of the family's food; why not make a good job of it and put something really wholesome and fine-flavoured on the table? What you can grow in your own garden is unobtainable in the shops. This book will not have fulfilled its purpose unless it has pointed beyond mere questions of cash-saving to the things that you can do to restore and preserve your physical well-being.

If all the available land at the front and back of people's houses in terms of lawns, flower beds, vegetable patches and space occupied by fruit trees were added together, a tremendous area would be covered. If this were placed under soundly-based biological cultivation, how valuable it would be with regard to health, not to speak of the monetary value! By providing part of our food supply on our own land, a great strain would be lifted from the environment – most of the fertilizer being obtained from the garden itself.

If you are still hesitating over whether or not to change to the type of biological gardening described here, I would ask you to consider the differences between the fruit and vegetables you buy and those you could be growing yourself, as far as flavour, digestibility and keeping quality are concerned. This is what should be meant when a good all-round diet is referred to. In addition to providing a satisfying and healthy basic diet, this type of vegetable garden allows us greater opportunities for avoiding denatured foods even when our occupations leave us little spare time for gardening.

In most gardens that are more than just status symbols, there are corners where the basic vegetables could be grown. When this has been attended to, the most important aim is to bring uncooked produce from the garden to the table at every meal. Raw fruit and vegetables are the foods with the widest range of action, the highest degree of curative power and the most astonishing nutritional value, when they are properly combined and prepared. They heal not only the disease but the entire organism, because they give it the strength to recover from its morbid condition. In this connection, I am not simply thinking of grated carrots, sliced beetroot and the like – the ordinary family needs more than these – no, the first thing to be thought of is the lettuce in all its forms, together with radishes, tomatoes, cucumbers, cress, endives and chicory. To these, grated carrots, beetroot and celery may, of course, be added; nor should we forget finely chopped spinach, stinging-nettles, garlic, salsify and Brussels sprouts. Who is to say that salads are only good for us when they are not seasoned or served with a dressing? Salads are both easy to prepare and delicious, and it is indeed true that we obtain most benefit from what we eat when we really enjoy it.

Garden Herbs for Daily Needs

Herbs are a valuable feature in the garden. They are in the truest sense of the words, 'the Lord God's homoeopathic dispensary'. Not only do they protect other plants from pests if wisely planted, but they also stand ready for our culinary needs.

Anyone who has read the previous chapters of this book will have come across the names of the following herbs at least once. I shall now examine them further, dealing with them separately as annuals and perennials. Herbs can also be divided into 'mild' and 'strong' when they are being considered for kitchen use.

Annual herbs:
Basil (*Ocimum basilicum*), borage, dill, parsley, marjoram (*Majorana hortensis*), chervil (*Anthriscus cerefolium*), purslain.

Use: These, plus one or two of the perennial herbs such as chives, tarragon, salad burnet, sorrel and lemon balm, are suitable for all salads, for eating on bread, for herb butter, for mixing with curd cheese, for herb soup and for sauces.

Perennial herbs:
Chives, tarragon, salad burnet, sorrel, lemon balm, lovage, summer savory, sage, thyme, mugwort (do not use the leaves but only the flowers), hyssop, rue, peppermint, lavender and rosemary (the latter is not a hardy plant but, nevertheless, it is not an annual).

In combination, no more than five to seven herbs should be used. With the exception of the first five, these herbs are very important for all dishes which are improved by having something to complement their flavour, and for all dishes which would kill the flavour of the milder herbs – which, in any case, should be eaten raw. They also help to make rich food more digestible. Examples are cummin (not listed above), which can usefully be grown next to plants of the cabbage family, and sage.

A selection of herbs should definitely be stored, in as wide a selection as you wish, for winter use: dill as flowers, cummin as ripe seeds, coriander as ripe seeds and mustard seed, together with the leaves of thyme, savory, sage, basil, tarragon, hyssop and rosemary.

Herbs were originally used as medicines, and even today are still used in this way to some extent. Since it is their food value which is to be considered here, I shall not go into the rights and wrongs of what has been said about them in other respects. Suffice it to say that every herb contains healing or prophylactic substances in homoeopathic doses. All herbs are remedial and contain minerals in assimilable form which are not as readily available elsewhere.

Medicinal and Nutritive Properties
It is well known that parsley contains more vitamin C than lemons do; that balm promotes sleep; that peppermint settles the stomach but is harmful to the eyes if taken every day; that sage and hyssop, in addition to being aids to digestion, are excellent remedies for sore throats and colds, in the first case for gargling, and in the second case as vapours giving almost instantaneous relief when inhaled – and so forth. I am not speaking here of wild herbs and berries which take time to gather and a certain amount of knowledge to identify. Neither am I referring to the various teas or tisanes which may be gathered from the fields or picked in one's own garden; something will be said of these in the section on herbal remedies and pot herbs on page 117.

Because we have planted them in our own garden, my family and I have a selection of herbs for everyday kitchen use which supplies everything the body needs in the way of trace elements etc., and all without extra expense. Knowing that parsley tea, for example, is particularly good for bladder trouble, more parsley should be used when the need arises. It should also be added to the liquid fertilizer. The same may be said of many other remedial teas, for example, bean pod tea as a diuretic. Why not include the bean pods in the plant material used to make the fertilizer brews? The results may be slower, but there seems to be no reason why they should not be just as sure.

When dealing with these important matters, it is vital to seize one's opportunities as they arise; instead of trying to avoid a little extra work, one should try to turn everything to advantage. One or two of the herbs make things easier since they stay green throughout the year; among them are sage, hyssop, perennial savory, thyme and, to some extent, salad burnet. Herbs are especially important in low-salt and salt-free diets. Special attention ought to be paid to the fact that any foodstuff (at any and every meal) is capable of carrying herbs and we should ensure that the latter are always available in the garden.

In some regions, it is traditional to grow a clump of chives in the garden; chives are rich in iron and vitamin A, they strengthen the stomach and make fatty foods (e.g. soups) digestible. Parsley is another favourite and besides giving an edge to the appetite, this is a useful diuretic. It can be used in almost all salads and vegetable dishes, in stuffings, with potatoes, in curd cheese and in many other dishes.

Dill is another useful addition to our meals. All parts of the plant are used. It helps in many disorders, is indispensable for making pickles and is especially important in a low-salt diet. Dill is still to be found in most gardens – so make sure you grow it yourself!

Fresh Salads
If the garden is cultivated as described in the foregoing pages, fresh produce will always be available for the table.

Lettuce
Always pick the lettuce just before eating and wash it quickly. Use sufficient salad dressing but not enough for any to be left behind in the bowl at the end of the meal. For children, the dressing should not be too sharp, but there should be no sugar in it.
Vary the dressings you use for your salads!
A well-tried favourite recipe is:
1 part vinegar, 1 part water or curdled milk, 2 parts vegetable oil, 5–7 salad herbs or onion, some curd cheese or *Quark** and yogurt, always with a little sea salt but no sugar. Do not overdo the wine vinegar, if this is the type used, as it is

*_Quark,_ which resembles the French *frommage blanc,* is now available in this country.

sharper. Have a little mild mustard to hand, but leave the usual run of condiments in the shop!

In spring, every one who has their own garden will want to put freshly cut cabbage lettuce on the table. However, cabbage lettuce has no surplus value. The later varieties of green salad plants with their light concentrations of bitter principles are more health-giving; corn salad for example contains twice as much vitamin C as cabbage lettuce does.

The daily green salad does need some flavouring in the form of herbs however: chives, marigold petals, chervil, balm, dill – all these improve and add the finishing touch to a salad.

Endives and chicory, which appear later, both containing bitter principles and, being especially helpful for biliousness, are forgotten just as often as is corn salad, and quite unjustly.

Endives and Sugarloaf

These are best served as whole leaves, i.e. *not* chopped up. Separate the leaves, wash them (to preserve the bitter principles use cold, never warm water) and arrange them in the bowl decoratively in an upright position. A yogurt dressing is a suitable accompaniment.

Corn Salad

The path which ran between the strawberries earlier in the year is ideal for sowing corn salad. The path was covered with straw and this should gradually have rotted down. The ground should be loosened and, if necessary, extra fertilizer should be added before scattering the seed over it. You will then have corn salad next to your strawberry plants, onions or leeks throughout the winter.

Corn salad may also be sown under individual trees and in similar places where the soil has been turned. After all, it grows wild in vineyards and meadows, so it does not require much care and attention.

Garden Cress

This is also important, since it has an antibiotic effect (bactericidal). It therefore makes an aggressive partner when sown with other plants. However, it is rich in vitamin C and is a cleanser of the system in gout and rheumatism. The cress you buy in the shops is brought on early for quick sales and contains less vitamin C.

All green salad plants, without exception, are meant to be eaten raw. There will always be something ready for the salad bowl if we remember to make repeated sowings of garden cress, mustard, various types of lettuce, endives and chicory plus Chinese cabbage.

Tomatoes and Cucumbers

These are good eaten raw. It is wise to avoid purchasing these vegetables when their place of origin is unknown. They go really well with herbs such as borage, dill, parsley and balm and, of course, with spring onions. Tomatoes contain vitamins A, B, C and many trace elements. They also give an edge to the appetite.

Tomatoes are good without vinegar but sometimes need a little sea salt, onions or herbs mixed with sour cream. Stir the dressing well, pour it over the tomatoes and allow the flavours to mingle.

Cucumbers are diuretic, they cleanse the kidneys, are cooling in fevers and relieve the heart and circulation by detoxication, help rheumatism and gout and improve the health of the skin (they act as a skin cleanser when applied externally). They are regarded as rather indigestible, but are easily digested, even at night, if thinly sliced and covered in vegetable oil and then, after some time, dressed with dill, borage, spring onions, a pinch of sea salt, vinegar and cream if preferred.

Radishes

These contain a lot of calcium and are of immediate benefit in liver trouble and biliousness. They are a first-rate cough remedy if a black winter-radish is scooped out and filled with sugar lumps to draw the juice. Radishes go very well with onions, and their value also depends on the way in which they are treated during cultivation. A salad of raw *Sauerkraut* is particularly good for diabetics; it is low in calorie content, it cleans the intestines and controls the intestinal flora.

Sauerkraut Salad

Mix together some *Sauerkraut* (page 114), spring onions, garlic, ground

---

Companion Planting in Beds

This illustration shows that companion planting is also possible in beds. The beds must be at least two metres wide and each bed should hold a self-contained group of companion plants, care being taken to get the composition right.

Nevertheless, cultivation in beds is not as satisfactory as the method already described that dispenses with paths and paving-stones. The positive influence from plants in neighbouring beds is reduced. When paving is put down, make sure that only the heat-loving varieties are planted next to the stones; for example, do not plant celery in such a position.

A big disadvantage of this method is the virtual impossibility of making compost *in situ*.

cummin, a little vegetable oil and mustard powder and allow the salad to stand for a short time. Place some grated apple underneath the salad to complement the flavour.

Sauerkraut Salad with Fruit

Raw *Sauerkraut* (page 114) with slices of orange, pineapple and bananas, peaches, apples and pears, fresh or bottled, according to the time of year. Some pear juice (from the bottle), some sloe or morello cherry juice. Mix the ingredients carefully but thoroughly. Do not add salt or sugar.

This makes a splendid *hors d'oeuvre*, but can also be eaten later in the meal.

Grated Salsify, Carrrot or Beetroot

These are improved by the addition of a little milk or cream, or finely chopped herbs and a squeeze of lemon juice. Season with coriander.

Celeriac Salad

Cook the celeriac, peel it and cut it into medium slices. Peel some apples and slice them finely. As a dressing mix together some finely chopped onions, sea salt, freshly ground black pepper, ground coriander, a little mustard, vinegar, vegetable oil, soured cream and stir well. Mix together the celery and apple and cover immediately with the dressing. Do not disturb as extra layers are added, just let the flavours of the dressing mingle. (Add a few slices of cooked parsnip, if liked).

Biennial and Perennial Herbs
The examples show cultivated forms of herbs, nearly all of which grow in the wild. The cultivated varieties retain their medicinal and seasoning properties.

Top left:
Perennial herbs can grow together in a herb bed or – even more suitable, since they act as a defence to other plants – can be planted in the round beds under rose-bushes for example.

Bottom left and bottom right:
Sage, lavender and hyssop used as a wall of protection for other plants.

Top right:
All herbs which become too 'woody' or have begun to fade when the flowering season is over can be used in the fermentation of liquid fertilizer. For special use they are put in piles according to species.

Raw Celeriac
This goes particularly well with grated apple or with grated red cabbage. 2 parts apple and 1 part celeriac should be well mixed with a silver fork. Alternatively, mix together 2 parts apple, 1 part celeriac and 1 part grated red cabbage.

Anyone who grows food for health can raise sound produce in his or her garden or can purchase it elsewhere, ought to invest in a juice extractor. It is necessary to ensure that food prepared in this way has not come into contact with any kind of toxic residues – the same applies to salads or any uncooked food. These vegetable juices are both nourishing and delicious, and when used regularly can make good the body's depleted reserves. In spring, for example, they will fortify the body against influenza, and they will do wonders for the convalescent. Nowadays, people are aware that a reduced vitamin intake in winter will lead to a jaded feeling in spring; however, this can be remedied by drinking the juices of beetroot, carrot and celery. By the addition of other juices, such as those extracted from apples and whole citrus fruit, the mixture is turned into a relish, a food and a fortifying medicine for small children. Although the amount given may be small, the nutrient value is great. Always supply a drinking straw, however, as this is better for the teeth and prevents the child from drinking too quickly.

Cooked Vegetables
All garden produce has healing as well as nutrient properties. Nevertheless, there are numerous pitfalls on the road from producing good organically grown vegetables to preparing equally wholesome meals. The full value is retained only when vegetables are picked in prime condition: that is to say, when beans have pods that snap open, when cauliflower heads are still tight, when garden peas are tender etc.

The goodness of fresh food is preserved if it is prepared by the shortest method and as quickly as possible. Freshness is an essential part of quality and of health-giving potential. The food should look tempting when placed on the table, since what looks and tastes good is appetizing and, in most cases, wholesome. The menu must of course vary according to the time of year.

In the past, the health-giving properties of vegetables have been under-valued, but this was because they were spoilt in the cooking, were over-processed, were not eaten raw often enough, and were impregnated with harmful chemicals. Vegetables were drowned in gravy, mixed with all sorts of unnecessary things and saturated with cooking fat. It is no use taking left-over vegetables (such as cauliflower, cabbage, potato and so on) to fry up as bubble-and-squeak in the hope that such a mishmash will have much health value. It bears repetition that food ought to be prepared as simply as possible, and that reprocessing or warming-up should be avoided.

If a thickening is required, rolled oats should be used instead of cornflour, because oats are so good for the health. Without having made a special study of the subject, it is difficult to say offhand the special virtues of various vegetables. Therefore it pays to cultivate as many species as possible, so that a varied diet with all sorts of health-giving properties can be provided. Since this is not a course on dietetics or cookery, I must content myself with one or two remarks on some of the more common vegetables. A reminder of the vegetables which go well together is added under each heading.

Any household with small children will find carrots important for nourishment, especially because they contain vitamin A. This benefits the nerves, the bone structure, the stomach and the intestines.

However, there is no sense in serving up carrots unless their quality is good: that is to say no fresh manure or toxic chemicals should have been used on them and they should have been harvested at the right time. These requirements can be guaranteed only when the carrots are organically grown at home or are purchased from a market garden run on sound biological lines. The same is true of course of other garden produce.

As with beetroots, more than one row of carrots should be growing at any one time.

Carrots
Rub all young carrots with sea salt, and wash but do not scrape them. Cut them into pieces of equal size, boil and toss them in steamed parsley and onions. Season with a pinch of sea salt. For a change, add some ground coriander or other herbs (see the section on herbs). A little milk or cream will improve the dish and make it more digestible.

Beetroot
This should never be omitted. It is best to sow the seed thinly in rows a few inches wide. The beetroot can then be pulled from one or another of the rows from summer onwards. Betroot should never be transplanted in the rows. This way they grow really big, it is true, but they then contain an exceptionally large amount of colouring matter.

Early in the season, the beetroot is a very juicy and tender vegetable. In fact, it is a good idea in summer to bottle it ready for winter while it is still young and soft. It can also be sliced into salads and can be steeped in vinegar. This is better than storing too many, since stored vegetables require over-long cooking time and thereby lose their goodness.

During summer, the housewife should remove the largest plants from the rows when they reach the size of small apples, and leave the others to grow further for winter needs. Even these beetroots should not be gathered too late, i.e. they have to be harvested while still tender. It is important to have several rows coming on in different stages of growth so that the beetroots are always ready for use.

The raw juice of beetroots (not drunk to quench the thirst but taken a spoonful at a time – if possible mixed with carrot and apple juice) is highly beneficial. Beetroot is a traditional tonic or pick-me-up and is a prophylactic against influenza. As any woman can quickly discover for herself, it improves the condition of the skin, and it soon invigorates pale, listless children.

Beetroot goes well with such biennial herbs as coriander and cummin, also with mustard powder and, naturally, with spring onions, but not with green herbs and, when made up in a salad, never with oil. To cook beetroot as a summer vegetable, boil them and peel the skins quickly under clear water; melt a little fat, lightly fry some finely chopped onions in it and toss the beetroot in the pan. Flavour with cummin and coriander.

Cabbage
Cabbage is the most important vegetable of all because it is such a cheap, staple food in so many households. Many gardeners also have room to spare to grow some extra cabbage for making their own *Sauerkraut*. Apart from this, however, cabbage is a first-rate medicinal plant. It is furnished with many vitamins, contains plenty of calcium and iron, but is properly effective medicinally only if it is grown with no excess of nitrogenous manure.

If you are going to make *Sauerkraut*, do use the cabbage from your own garden. This is an ideal food for diabetics, is also low in calories, cleans the intestines and regulates the bacterial flora to be found in them. The raw juice from your home-made *Sauerkraut* is an untouched natural product, a valuable health food.

According to the method of preparation, cabbages of any kind go well with onions, dill seed, cummin, apples, juniper berries and various herbs.

White Cabbage/Savoy Cabbage
For best results, boil whole or halved and sliced as for kohlrabi (see above).

Red Cabbage
Slice some red cabbage, onions and apples and place them in layers with a little vegetable oil, cummin or juniper berries, adding a pinch of sea salt and a tablespoonful of vinegar or wine according to taste. Before serving, instead of the usual sugar, add some unsweetened raspberry juice or a tablespoonful of black currant jelly, but no flour.

'Bavarian' Cabbage

For this recipe, the cabbage is usually cooked with flour in fat, a mixture that easily burns. It is better to treat it like red cabbage (above), but without the juice or jelly, merely adding a little wine.

Sauerkraut Recipe

Sauté some onions in vegetable oil until the flavour has developed, add unwashed and undrained home-made *Sauerkraut* which has properly fermented (see page 114), and immediately pour boiling water over the top until the *Sauerkraut* is covered. Do not add salt, but top with sliced apple, juniper berries, cummin and more onions. Cover the pan and simmer for about 1 hour without stirring. Place some greaseproof paper between the lid and the pan, and do not remove it until the dish is cooked. For those who like some thickening, grate a small raw potato and stir it into the mixture. (Incidentally, it is not advisable to warm food up too often after the first serving).

Cauliflower

Boil the cauliflower and then add a knob of butter, melted herb butter or some wholemeal breadcrumbs in butter.

Kohlrabi

Cook the kohlrabi whole, then slice it into disks (without completely severing them), put some herb butter between each slice or, instead of butter, onion and curd cheese mixed (see recipe on page 107).

Kale

Boil the kale and remove the tough stalk; stew plenty of onions in vegetable stock until soft, but do not fry them. Lay strips of kale over the onions, add grated cheese to taste and some soured milk. Cover the pan and allow the flavours to mingle.

Potatoes

Make a point of growing potatoes in your own garden or in a small allotment. Potatoes are more than just a filling food; they have a neutralizing and diuretic action, and help to prevent deficiency diseases. Potatoes are especially valuable in cases of gout, rheumatism, scurvy, and in fluid retention due to heart disease. The raw juice has been recommended by doctors for hyper-acidity of the stomach, and hot potato has been prescribed for compresses applied to the throat. Fried potato should be avoided; so should preparations using fat and flour.

Although they can be prepared in so many different ways, it is a well-known fact that potatoes are best for health when baked in their jackets. However, since most of the vital ingredients are retained in cooking, the mode of preparation may be varied fairly freely. In fact, the potato is a vegetable which is not sufficiently valued as a daily food. It is important as a source of minerals – iron, potassium, calcium and phosphorus. The versatility of this vegetable is increased by the variety of herbs which may be used with the various potato dishes.

Note: The more processing the vegetable undergoes, the more its health value is diminished.

1. *Peeled Potatoes*
   a) Sieved boiled potatoes, dotted with butter without any other addition or preparation;
   b) Mashed potatoes (milk and butter mixed in with a fork or masher);
   c) Potato salad (vegetable oil added);
   d) Potato dumplings.

2. *Baked Potatoes;* when cooked, split the skins of the potato and scoop out the flesh.

3. Potatoes in their Jackets; cut raw new potatoes in half, dip the cut surfaces in sea salt and cummin, place the potatoes on a baking tray, sprinkled with a little vegetable oil if desired. Bake until soft inside and eat the potatoes with the skins on.

4. *To Peel Potatoes;* wash them, dip them in cold water, then place them in boiling water for a few minutes until the peels can be removed easily. The potatoes will then be clean and white and ready to cook.
   Creamed potato is made by boiling some salted potatoes until almost cooked (the water can be used in a soup); pour on some soured cream, and add a knob of fresh butter to improve the taste. Allow the flavours to mingle in the saucepan with the lid off. You will then have a satisfying meal with a great flavour.

Spinach
Although spinach is grown in the companion-planted garden for more than kitchen use, it ought to be included in the small selection of vegetables discussed here, since it can be proved that, even with a so-called biological fertilizer (i.e. a fertilizer made of natural ingredients), overmanuring in this case can be just as serious as with chemical nitrates. In either case, the dose is what matters. A test bed purposely overmanured with an organic fertilizer gave large, dark green

leaves which, although they may have looked attractive, tasted pretty dreadful.

Spinach, which contains very valuable, not to say indispensable substances, needs careful treatment, and the spinach rows in the companion-planted garden should never be manured. This plant is very important in nutrition: it stimulates the liver, gall-bladder and the digestion; it helps to make blood, contains vitamin A as well as half a dozen other vitamins and plenty of iron. Figwort and dandelion are useful supplementary herbs.

Spinach leaves are especially good when mixed with onions, herbs and butter, then eaten raw or steamed or made into a fine *purée*. Spinach, stinging-nettle and sorrel make a good combination, eaten alone or else mixed with corn salad, garlic, onions, vinegar and vegetable oil.

Celeriac

As we have already seen in the chapter on growing mixed crops, celeriac should never be absent from a companion-planted garden. In terms of nutrition it is outstanding as a 'nerve food'. It is remarkably good diuretic and indispensable as part of a low-salt diet. The tuber, stalk and leaf are all beneficial here. It may be mixed with milder vegetables to tone down its strong flavour if this is not appreciated.

Except when used as a seasoning for stews etc., celeriac is generally regarded exclusively as a salad plant, which is a great pity. Slices of celeriac fried in vegetable oil, are worth trying, as are stuffed celeriac roots, so that this vegetable could be eaten more often. (For its use in vegetable broths see pages 107 and 108).

Parsnips

These are a particularly good accompaniment for celeriac, and so are courgettes and, of course, potatoes. Parsnips, courgettes and celeriac are all suitable for a diabetic diet. A particularly delicious salad is one made of celeriac cooked with parsnips, to which is added for extra goodness spring onions, marigold petals and sliced apples. This is dressed with a little vinegar, vegetable oil and fresh cream. In this way, the cooked salad is improved by raw garnishing.

While we are on the subject of cooked salads, it should be emphasized how important it is to add raw vegetables to them, especially spring onions and garlic. They are then enhanced rather than devalued foods.

Beans

Kidney beans and runner bean plants should be grown mainly for the beans themselves; these have a high protein content and a marked diuretic action, thus relieving the heart. The ripe beans (not the pods) are used to treat the skin condition known as erythema; bean flour is used as a cosmetic. The dried pods are also important, and can be used for bean pod tea. These are also one of the key ingredients in the vegetable broth (page 108) made from whatever vegetables happen to be ready in the garden, enriched with herbs, the above-mentioned bean pods and also pea pods.

Fruit and Berry Crops

Top left:
Tomatoes in early summer. The first side-fruit has been picked; the crop now requires more room. The undersown mustard is providing cover at the base of the tomato plant. The leaves are necessary as nutriment.

Top right:
Raspberries (Romy) are the main crop of an autumn-fruiting variety up to the first frosts. As with the wild raspberry, it is not susceptible to spur blight. Growing conditions should be similar to those found in woodlands with some shade and covered soil. Use straw as litter only for raspberry and strawberry plants (below).

Bottom:
The resulting strawberry crop one year after onions have been planted as neighbouring plants. Straw keeps the crop clean and these fruit do not need washing. When the straw rots down it provides a favourable place for the strawberry runners.

Top left:
Half-made compost was spread at the base of this young apple tree in winter. At the start of new growth, undiluted liquid nettle fertilizer was applied and a medicinal herb, in this case mustard, was undersown. Nasturtium is another companion plant for this type of tree.
Disadvantage: comes up later because it is sensitive to frost.
Advantages: suppresses couch-grass and discourages aphides. Marigolds are another option.

Top right:
An old apple tree, damaged several times during building operations, but restored by care of the trunk (see page 00).

Bottom:
Reine-Claude greengages treated with 'home-grown' manure; this tree produces a consistent crop of firm fruit and the yield is high. All the fruit trees bear sound fruit with good keeping qualities.

Preparing Dried Beans

Wash the beans, soak them in plenty of cold water then cook them slowly in the water in which they have been soaked. The following ingredients towards the end of the cooking time: onions, garlic, whole cummin, whole juniper berries, parsley, a little horse-radish (when available), sage and, if possible, a few dried bean pods. A little fat may be added if so desired but this is usually unnecessary.

Companion Planting Flowers

This is a community of flowering plants which, at first sight, appears to have been put together on aesthetic grounds. All the plants from the annuals to the perennials are medicinal. The roses are a good substitute for the wild species and old-fashioned garden varieties, and have known active constituents. All the other flowers have had a place in cottage gardens for centuries and all are still employed in herbal medicine, either when added to the regular diet or as infusions (herbal teas); for instance, balm, mullein, marigold. On the other hand, all the plants have a value in helping to provide a healthy and protective environment for the community as a whole.

Top left:
A wild hedgerow.
Cow-parsnip in the foreground, backed by lilac, buckthorn (*Hippophae rhamnoides*), elder and other early-flowering shrubs – all of which made a windbreak in the old country gardens.

In addition, the medicinal herb comfrey is visible, as well as soil-covering Chinese lanterns (*Physalis alkekengi*) and an undergrowth of dead-nettles. A few stinging-nettles should also be allowed to take their place here and there in the undergrowth as many species of butterfly rely on them.

Top right:
Old-fashioned roses of various sorts are planted in beds of two metres wide. All have a powerful scent. Dittany (*Dictamnus albus*), which is also a woodland plant is put in with them too. All beds are edged with the usual herbs, also with box (*Buxus*). (*Arctostaphylos uva-ursi*). Shredded organic material (see page 41) is used as a manure. The attractive blue flowers of phacelia, to which bees are always attracted, can be seen underneath the roses. Beside the paving stones are planted the heat-loving herbs such as low-growing thyme and purslain.

Bottom:
This luxuriant growth of healthy flowers was not achieved by close planting but by manuring exclusively with the garden's own fermented liquid compost, by loosening the soil with a hoe and by spreading chopped organic material round the base of the plants. This provides favourable conditions for semi-woodland plants such as roses, Turk's cap, dittany, and also for Madonna and tiger lilies.

The broth is strained and ready for serving after the pods have been removed and everything else has been sieved. Do not add any thickening.

Lentils, which may also be grown in the garden, are prepared in the same way.

Flageolets
These may be cooked with parsley and onions, but also summer savory, spoonwort and sorrel. Although dried beans are regarded as indigestible, this is not the case if they are cooked with onions and summer savory and also, if possible, with garlic, thyme, sage, horse-radish (*Cochlearia armoracia*), juniper berries (*Juniperus communis*), tarragon, lovage and mugwort. A selection of these herbs (which are mainly biennial) may be used according to the time of year.

Peas
Young green peas are very good, but need other herbs such as spoonwort, sorrel, parsley and onions with them to improve the effect. It is also important to dry the green pods for use in vegetable soups as described for bean pods.

Peas, as suppliers of protein, may also be used when fully mature: cook them with such herbs as thyme, sage, celery, cummin and summer savory (see the section on dried beans above). Fresh peas should be boiled briefly and mixed with some *sautéed* parsley and onions.

Green and Red Peppers
These have a very high vitamin C content. They may be served raw in a salad, *sautéed* as a separate vegetable or filled with rice. Peppers need more heat when growing than tomato plants do and they are usually imported.

Chicory
This can also be grown in the garden, but care must be taken to lift the whole plant including the root, to pot it in earth or sand and to put it in a cool dark place. It will then keep as a good winter salad or winter vegetable. Chicory may be served steamed with little in the way of garnishing, or as a salad with yogurt dressing as for endives and sugar-loaf.

Onions
These should never be absent from any garden, however small. The chapter on page 11 describes how to cover the needs of the household the whole year through. Onions are indispensable in the kitchen. They strengthen the gastric nerves, act as appetizers, cleansers of the system (like garlic) and have a

favourable action on high blood pressure. They also destroy bacteria. Onions disinfect, reduce the level of blood sugar and help damaged skin. They also improve the condition of the hair and should be used daily in some form or other. Since the valuable substances contained in the onion are heat-resistant, onions do not have to be eaten raw in order to have their optimum effect. Herbs which complement onions – according to the type and form of the meal – are parsley, dill, balm, sage, savory and marigold petals.

If the right varieties are chosen and put in at the proper times, sufficient onions will be available right through the winter. The keeping properties of onions depend on methods of cultivation, varieties, and also on the fact that onions must never be watered or manured. There are indeed many reasons, besides the beneficial effect on the other plants with which it is grown, for cultivating the onion in one's own garden.

Onions have a time-honoured place in all salads and also in cooked dishes. Yet some varieties of onion are relatively unknown. The shallot is a case in point. This fine-flavoured vegetable should be skinned and then boiled until soft. Prepare a light batter with the water in which they were boiled and a little flour mixed with melted vegetable fat. Remove the pan from the heat and add some milk, cream or egg yolk with a little lemon juice before serving over the shallots.

Large onions are best steamed, then sieved to make a *purée* and then steamed a little longer.

Onion Cheese
Stir together equal quantities of curd cheese and finely chopped onions, with a pinch of sea salt, mustard powder, a clove of garlic (crushed) and a little milk or soured cream. Make sure that the mixture is thick (it should not drop easily from the spoon).

Leeks
Leeks are particularly good boiled whole (save the liquid for broth or soup), topped with wholemeal breadcrumbs in butter or some soured milk and baked for a short time in the oven.

Vegetable Broths and Soups
It will probably be obvious by now that, in my opinion, nothing can take the place of garden produce, both as food and as a source of good health. I regard it as the indispensable foundation of our diet, and I should like to give a recipe here which is extremely important as far as nutrition is concerned: this is a

recipe for so-called vegetable broth. When carefully made, this extracts all the goodness from the vegetables and is therefore a concentrate of the highest value and finest flavour, which – without the addition of fat – may be given to small children. It also has valuable healing properties. It has nothing in common with the so-called 'vegetable meat broth', which is usually thick and tasteless. Vegetable broth can be made throughout summer and autumn, and in winter too if the right vegetables have been put in store; this means that the bottled produce can be mixed and enriched with whatever is still growing in the garden at that season or has been stored in sand in the cellar (or a similar cool, dark place).

It is true that soups are often avoided, mostly because they are thought to be fattening. But there is no reason why the body's fluid requirements should not be met in part by a small bowlful of such concentrated broth. If you want to put something into the broth to give it body, use brown rice, green rye, flaked oats, pearl barley and the like.

There is no need to begrudge the many vegetables used in making the broth. If properly prepared, any left-over broth can be eaten instead of cooked vegetables or else steamed and turned into a *purée*. However, the main goodness is in the broth itself.

Vegetable Broth
A little vegetable oil
2 onions, coarsely chopped
1 stick celery, halved
2–3 leeks, sliced lengthways
Celery leaves
4–6 carrots
3 parsley roots (turnip-rooted parsley)
Extra parsley leaves
3–4 tomatoes
½ cauliflower (or the stalk and clean leaves)
1 white cabbage, quartered
1 kohlrabi, halved
Handful each of fresh beans,
    peas (with pods), dried pea
    and bean pods (from winter store)
1–2 lovage leaves
Pinch each of basil and sea salt (optional)
In a large saucepan, *sauté* the vegetables in the oil and then cover them with water. Allow the broth to simmer gently over a low heat without stirring it. (The vegetables should become soft but should not disintegrate.)

Egg Soup with Wholewheat Bread and Broth
Lightly stir 1 oz (25g) butter over a low heat and add 4 oz (100g) wholemeal breadcrumbs (stale). Break 2 eggs into the mixture and add some vegetable broth (page 108). Allow the soup to stand and then bring to the boil.

Cream of Herb Soup
Cook some finely chopped herbs in vegetable oil, add some vegetable broth (page 108) and boil well. Thicken the soup with some soured cream and 1 egg yolk.

Referring back to what has already been said about the value of various vegetables, the value of making vegetable broths becomes obvious. The cooked vegetables mentioned, and others besides, e.g. salsify, asparagus, dried beans and lentils, can also be used in salads. Here, the raw items, such as spring onions and herbs, enhance the health value of the cooked items.

Cooking with Fruit

Strawberries
When eaten raw, strawberries are – according to Kneipp – a good vermifuge; they contain organic acids and require the addition of sugar when made into jam. For this reason, they should be eaten raw whenever possible. This applies both to children and to adults, particularly those who are overweight and would appreciate the low calorie content of this fruit. Strawberries act as a body cleanser, are good for the liver and gall-bladder and are also diuretic.

Damsons
The laxative substances in damsons retain their potency even when cooked (a main advantage of this fruit), and damson jam may be eaten by the spoonful.

Damson Jam
I. Place 6 lb (3 kilos) damsons and 1 lb (½ kilo) raw cane sugar in a saucepan overnight and, on the following day, boil the fruit and sugar over a low heat. Do not stir the jam as damsons cook in their own juice. Remove the pan from the heat and stir well for 15 minutes. Pour the jam into ovenproof containers and place them in the oven at a low temperature until a leathery skin forms on the surface.
II. Place ¾ lb (350g) raw cane sugar in a saucepan and heat it gently until lumps are formed (do not allow to burn). Add the damsons and stir them until the sugar is dissolved. Cook for half an hour, remove the saucepan from the heat, and stir the jam for 15 minutes.

Peaches, mirabelle plums, greengages and apricots can also be made into jam following this recipe.

Apples

This fruit is indispensable. Apples have a high vitamin C content, help to prevent sclerosis of the arteries, reduce the cholesterol in the blood, and have a tannin content that inhibits inflammation.

The apple is a classic health fruit. It relieves the strain on the heart and circulation and contains many important minerals and trace elements. It can be used in many ways to make good the deficiencies in some other foods. Apples complement less digestible foods such as red cabbage and *Sauerkraut* (see page 114); apples also go well with celery in a salad. (There are countless variations and recipes for this fruit). Avoid imported apples since these are hardly ever very fresh and home-grown apples are more health-giving than any others.

In addition to fruit trees, room should be made in the garden for the various berries: the raspberry is an old medicinal plant with the richest active principles, and gooseberries are good for weak nerves and for anaemia.

The garden should also have a space for red currants and black currants, with their high vitamin A and C content. These, especially the black currants, provide stamina. A blackberry hedge, too, will provide fruit with a very high vitamin C content.

In winter, the place of fresh garden fruit is taken by juices, jellies and other preserves, which are particularly popular with children.

Although it is best to avoid using sugar as far as possible, a certain amount is needed to make winter berries palatable. Nevertheless, the pound-for-pound rule observed in ordinary jam recipes should be ignored. The sugar content must be kept low and the cooking time short. To keep, bottle the fruit and sterilize for a further 10 minutes at 158°F (70°C). However, this is not possible with jellies, so here is a little-known recipe for this type of jam.

Raspberry and Blackcurrant Jam

4½ lb (2¼ kilos) of black currants, not topped and tailed, are washed, quickly drained, and cooked in a pan until the skins burst. Pass 1 lb (½ kilo) of fresh raspberries through a wide hair-sieve (approx. 12 in.) and pour them over the stewing black currants. While the fruit is cooking, clarify 3 lb (1½ kilos) of raw cane sugar in just over ½ pint (¼ litre) of water and boil it until ropy or viscid. Run the juice that has been extracted from the fruit into the boiling sugar solution, remove from the heat and immediately stir for 4–5 minutes. Pour the jam into jars.

I should now like to mention three wild fruit which are also commonly found in gardens: the extremely valuable sloe, elder and rose hip. Hips have a high vitamin C content and so should be prepared carefully.

Elder Juice
Reduce the berries to a juice in the following way: Add 7 oz (200g) of raw cane sugar to 10 lb (300g) of elder fruit. Bottle and seal immediately (while boiling). Drink the juice hot when suffering from a heavy cold!

Sloe Juice
Pour boiling water over the sloes, leave them to stand for 1 day, then decant the deep red juice. (The more sloes the better). Add ½ lb (¼ kilo) of raw cane sugar to 2 pints (1 litre) of juice and boil the mixture for several minutes. Pour the boiling liquid into hot bottles and cork immediately. This is very good when added to puddings and trifles, to raw *Sauerkraut* salad (page 00), and as a drink (diluted with mineral water).

Rose Hip Pulp
I. Take 2 pints (1 litre) of rose hips (with the pips removed) and ¼ pint (150ml) of wine or water and keep the mixture in a covered vessel in a cool, dark place for 6–8 days; stir occasionally and sieve. To 1 lb (½ kilo) of pulp, add ¾ lb (350g) of raw cane sugar and cook until a suitable consistency is achieved.
II. For 1 lb (½ kilo) of thick pulp, 1 lb (½ kilo) of raw cane sugar is clarified in ¼ pint (150ml) of water. Add the pulp to the sugar, bring to the boil, place the mixture in a bowl and stir until cold. If the pulp is thin, bring 1 lb (½ kilo) of pulp and 1 lb (½ kilo) of ground raw cane sugar to the boil, then stir until cold as before.

Sauces and Dressings

Curd Cheese Dressing for Hard-boiled Eggs
Mix some curd cheese with the usual condiments and add chives, finely chopped spinach leaves, chervil, borage, parsley, vinegar and plenty of vegetable oil.

Yogurt Salad Dressing
This is a particularly fine salad dressing, which can be used on cooked and raw salads. Combine the following ingredients:
1 carton natural yogurt
1 onion, chopped
Pinch of sea salt
2 teaspoonsful mustard
1 tablespoonful cider vinegar
2–3 tablespoonsful vegetable oil
A little soured cream
1 tablespoonful tomato mustard (page 113)
Pinch of mustard powder
1–2 tablespoonsful black currant jelly
(Do not add any herbs)

'Green' Sauce for Potatoes
Sieve or mash 4 hard-boiled egg yolks and stir in some sea salt, vinegar, black pepper and vegetable oil. Add a little garlic and plenty of herbs such as chives, borage, dill, basil, tarragon, salad burnet, sorrel, and balm, and mix in natural yogurt or your own soured cream until thick. (Curd cheese may be used instead of cream).

Vegetable Gravy
Take some carrots, tomatoes and plenty of onions and herbs, chop them up roughly and fry them in some vegetable oil over a slow heat until dark yellow or light brown. If desired, a little cornflour can be mixed in and quickly cooked in the fat; then everything is covered with water and allowed to cook slowly over a low heat. (Do not cover). The gravy will go on cooking under a thin layer of fat. Season to taste. Home-made tomato sauce or tomato mustard (page 113) will go well with this too.

It is not generally known that by using certain vegetables and herbs, it is possible to make a 'vegetable gravy'. This can be a great help to anyone who has a garden in which the basic ingredients are grown.

Stocking Up for Winter
It is sensible to prepare for the winter months before the end of the year draws in. The growing season is never really over in the garden; even when snow is on the ground, there are still Brussels sprouts, kale, leeks, corn salad (lamb's lettuce), one or two herbs, sugar loaf and perhaps some winter spinach. But how can the gardener ensure all-round nourishment for the winter?

Bottling and Preserving

A start is made with winter preparations at the time when the first peas are being picked. The pods are kept and dried (see the sections on dried peas and on vegetable broth, pages 106 and 107). Any of the early varieties which quickly run to seed or become overripe or burst their skins etc. should, if they cannot be eaten quickly, be deep frozen. The first white cabbage can be made into *Sauerkraut* (see page 114). *Beetroot is bottled (sliced or whole), kohlrabi are cooked, sliced and deep frozen, *carrots are bottled, spinach is deep frozen and so on. Although I realize that it is best to eat produce as soon as it is picked, we must also endeavour to preserve the surplus in some way, remembering that most produce that can be stewed may also be bottled. Early non-keeping varieties of apple which do not store well, for instance, will make an excellent *compote* (served with lemon juice). Everything else, such as outside leaves of vegetables, which is clean and healthy, can be made into a broth and bottled.

Onions, garlic and shallots are gathered, dried and packed in bundles. By late summer and autumn we have the last of the tomatoes which, if ripened artificially, possess little goodness. It is better to make them into tomato *purée*, to deep freeze them or to bottle them. Halved tomatoes taken from the deep-freeze cabinet are useful for many purposes during the depths of winter.

Tomato Mustard

10 lb (5 kilos) of chopped tomatoes, 1 pint (½ litre) of wine vinegar, 10 level tablespoonsful of sea salt, 6 tablespoonsful of raw cane sugar, ¼ oz (7g) of whole ginger, 6 cloves, 6 bay leaves, 12 chopped onions, a good pinch of paprika, 1 cupful of mustard seed, 1 large sprig of thyme, basil, tarragon or savory and, when available, 1 green pepper. Cook the ingredients until soft in their own juice, sieve the mixture and boil it down over a low heat until thick. Keep the mustard in small earthenware pots; it can also be bottled and is splendid for improving and enriching cooked dishes and also as a relish with various salads.

Pickling

Very early in summer one should start thinking about the winter's supply of vitamins in the form of 'lactic acid' vegetables such as *Sauerkraut* (page 114) and gherkins. Gherkins may be pickled right through the summer and, in this way, you can be certain that there are always some in prime condition until

Note: During the war, the Ministry issued warnings against domestic bottling of root vegetables because of the danger from lethal soil organisms if sterilization was inadequate.

spring. Both vegetables are packed with vitamins and are indispensable during winter. Gherkins go well with many different meals, and *Sauerkraut* may be served cooked or raw or as an ingredient in some other dish. The following recipe uses ingredients which have already been recommended as promoters of health and as disinfectant or bactericidal in their action.

Pickled Gherkins

Take an earthenware pot and line the bottom with black currant leaves, then cover them with a layer of green gherkins, 4–5 inches long; (wash the gherkins well and soak them for several hours in clear water beforehand). Cover the gherkins with a layer of all sorts of herbs and spices, namely black peppercorns, 1–2 cloves, 1 bay leaf, plenty of dill flowers, tarragon, salad burnet, savory, sage, basil, thyme, 1 handful of shallots, horse-radish, some cloves of garlic, 1 small diced celeriac and 1 tablespoonful of mustard seed. Repeat these layers until the pot is filled. Place black currant leaves on top. Pour on a solution of 3½ pints (1¾ litres) of water, 1 pint (½ litre) of wine vinegar and 7 oz (200g) of sea salt.

Home-made Sauerkraut (without salt)

Line the bottom of a large earthenware pot with clean cabbage leaves, then compress layer after layer of the chopped cabbage very thoroughly, and finally cover with cabbage leaves and weight down with the usual stone. On the same day, pour on boiled water that has been cooled to 107.5°F (42°C). (The water must cover everything). On the next day, take a look and, if necessary, top up with water.

Following fermentation, which is pure lactic acid fermentation, cover with a linen cloth instead of the cabbage leaf and keep the contents weighted down. Because it is a pure lactic acid product, *Sauerkraut* is sensitive to the way it is treated; therefore the quality of the pot and the use of a clean linen cloth is all-important. The liquid must always cover the cabbage – as little air as possible must reach the vegetable matter. So cover well with a lid and clean cloth which can be placed over the whole pot. Even with ordinary earthenware pots it is not necessary to wash as often as is always recommended. What is more, if you use *Sauerkraut* daily for cooking or making salads, or for its raw juice, a lot of unnecessary washing and rinsing is avoided.

Storing Root Crops

Storing root crops for the winter is much more difficult. There would be no problem if every house still had a good cellar. If you have a cellar, then store the surplus root crops there after drying them well in the garden. The best thing to put them in is sand. A chest can be used for the purpose but the cellar floor is better. If this method is out of the question, there are two other possibilities: a) Put the roots in old earthenware pots – (dry the vegetables well and remove any earth with the hands). Wrap them in plenty of newspaper (not in tin foil). A certain amount of decay is to be expected, but the top layers of vegetables will be sound.

b) The roots can be packed in plastic bags such as are used in the deep-freeze cabinet. In this case, however, particular care must be taken to see that the produce is perfect. Celeriac, for example, must not be frost-bitten. Carrots ought to be smooth and should be harvested at the right time.

When root vegetables are harvested, they must first be left to dry where they are. Then the leaves are twisted off. The roots are taken to the place where they will be stored for the winter, e.g. to the cellar. Later on, they have to be cleaned (without a brush), and bagged up in open plastic sacks. After they have reached the temperature of the room in which they are stored, the plastic sacks are tied shut but a few holes are made with a needle. Make extra holes if you see any condensation inside the plastic. No method is 100 per cent perfect, especially since the different crops vary in their keeping qualities (there is no problem for example, with beetroot) and react in different ways; but this method goes some way in providing sufficient winter vegetable juices and raw produce.

Keeping Herbs

Many writers recommend deep-freezing herbs and also give recipes for preserving them with salt. The latter practice must be avoided at all costs – we consume more than enough cooking salt as it is. Deep-freezing certainly overcomes this difficulty, but the question remains as to whether the altered flavour of deep-frozen parsley, for instance, is still satisfactory.

It is preferable to pot up parsley and to stand the pots on the kitchen window-sill. This can be done even in late winter, because parsley can be brought in from the garden in the snow. Chives can also be potted in autumn and regularly be brought into the kitchen to sprout fresh leaves. However, before this is done, the chives must have had a touch of frost! Quite often, the plant will be attacked by aphides since it is being grown in abnormal conditions. The only thing to do in this case is to put it out of doors again and possibly to replant it.

Drying

Drying was at one time widely practised but it does have certain drawbacks (such as loss of vitamins etc.). However, dried vegetables keep well and are still very useful in this condition. They should be dried in the shade as far as is possible (in a loft, say). Drying ovens may also be used. Oil-burning ovens are available nowadays for slow drying, and the results obtained are very satisfactory. Herbs, slices of celeriac and their leaves, tomato halves (placed on wire cake racks), pea and bean pods, stoned plums and halved pears are all suitable for drying. All dried vegetables should be stored in small bags (if possible of linen), which are then hung up in an airy place.

An ABC of Medicinal and Culinary Herbs

Balm (*Melissa officinalis*)
Medicinal effect: tranquillizing, taken for insomnia; expectorant and good for the stomach and intestines.
Application: spirit of balm.
Cosmetic use: for face compresses, as a sedative bath.
Culinary use: with all uncooked food, in all fresh salads, in vegetable soups and gravies.

Basil (*Ocimum basilicum*)
Medicinal effect: aids digestion, sudorific, good against flatulence; helps in troubles of the bladder, kidneys and bile.
Application: a tea (tisane), given cold for fevers.
Culinary use: as a fine flavouring for all raw and cooked foods, for salads, cooked vegetables, gravies.
Cosmetic use: as a steam vapour.

Beans
Medicinal effect: the liquid in which they have been boiled is strongly diuretic.
Cosmetic use: the tea may be used as a face cleanser. Bean flour can be used in a face pack.

Borage (*Borago officinalis*)
Medicinal effect: its potassium content gives it diuretic and diaphoretic properties. The flowers act as a heart tonic. The roots supply a remedy for diseases of the skin and mucous membranes. The plant is blood purifying.

Application: fresh leaves are mixed with other herbs. The flowers are employed in tisanes.
Culinary use: in uncooked foods, salads, curd and cheese, vegetable soups and gravies. Suitable for a low-salt diet.

Burnet saxifrage (*Pimpinella saxifraga*)
Medicinal effect: strongly detoxicating, especially good for the liver and gall bladder, the stomach and intestines. Also stimulates the appetite and benefits the respiratory organs.
Application: the fresh leaves are used.
Culinary use: in soups and gravies and with all kinds of uncooked foods, curd cheese etc.

Caraway (*Carum carvi*)
Effect and use as for coriander.

Celery (*Apium graveolens*)
Medicinal effect: the leaf, stalk and root are all used and are especially good against fluid retention, gout and rheumatism, acting as a diuretic.
Application: raw or cooked, as a juice (blended), and dried.
Culinary use: in any savoury meal; in broths, soups, as a vegetable, in salads, raw or cooked. In low-salt diets.

Chervil (*Anthriscus cerefolium*)
Medicinal effect: blood purifying, diuretic, calmative; aids digestion.
Application: used either fresh or dried.
Culinary use: in soups and gravies especially in spring; in uncooked food, curd cheese etc.

Chives (*Allium*)
Medicinal effect: helps to reduce high blood pressure; acts as an appetizer, digestive; is beneficial to the kidneys and veins.
Application: use fresh.
Culinary use: used regularly in all broths and soups, in sandwiches, salad dressings and egg dishes.

Coriander (*Coriandrum sativum*)
Medicinal effect: strengthens the stomach and intestines; is an appetizer, good for the liver and antispasmodic.
Application: the dried seeds are eaten; the oil is used in embrocations.

Culinary use: with cabbages and potatoes, in breads, with beetroot, in uncooked food, in curd cheese, with all heavy and fatty meals. Used ground and as whole seeds.

Cress: Garden cress, Indian cress, (Nasturtium), Watercress (*Nasturtium officinale*)

Medicinal effect: high vitamin C content. Good for the stomach and intestines and against infections.

Application: the fresh leaves are used – before flowering in the case of nasturtiums!

Culinary use: eaten raw, either on their own or in salads. Nasturtium seeds can be preserved in vinegar and used instead of capers. Cress, especially watercress, should be avoided during pregnancy.

Dill (*Anethum graveolens*)

Medicinal effect: acts as a galactagogue (encouraging the secretion of milk), stimulates the glands, good against indigestion (used as an infusion for infants with 'wind'), against flatulence, colic (griping pains), and insomnia. Lowers the blood sugar level. Dill is a valuable food supplement.

Application: the fresh leaves, the flowers and the seeds are all used. Besides its use as a seasoning, dill is prepared as a tea.

Culinary use: the fresh leaves or the seeds are used with vegetables of all sorts (cauliflower, Brussels sprouts, asparagus, salsify, green beans); used in soups and sauces, with potatoes, in uncooked food, curd cheese etc. Dill flowers are indispensable for pickling gherkins, and are boiled to prepare an ingredient of salad dressings. Should be used freely in diabetes. Suitable for low-salt diets.

Fennel (*Foeniculum vulgare*)

Medicinal effect: has a beneficial action on the bronchi and lungs and in coughs. Good for obstructions of the gall-bladder. Promotes milk formation.

Application: the seeds are used as a tea. The main plant is used as a vegetable, the leaves as a fine flavouring for savoury dishes. The seeds, together with those of anise, cummin and coriander are used to prepare an extract which makes an excellent cough remedy when mixed with honey.

Culinary use: the seeds are added to beetroot; the main plant is used as a vegetable. The powdered seeds are mixed with raw carrot and the leaves are used like dill leaves to give a fine flavour.

Cosmetic use: fennel tea with honey, curd cheese and fuller's earth may be used as a face pack.

Garlic (*Allium sativum*)

Medicinal effect: acts as a disinfectant, inhibits putrefactive bacteria, prevents hardening of the arteries, counteracts high blood pressure; garlic is blood purifying, promotes the circulation of the blood and regulates the intestinal flora.

Application: use daily as a seasoning, often combined with parsley. This may be taken in powdered form.

Culinary use: raw in salads, soups, vegetable stews, herb butter and in many condiments; it is important for pickles (preserves well), and for use with gherkins etc.

Horse-radish (*Cochlearia armoracia*)

Medicinal effect: acts as an appetizer, digestive, diuretic, helps the liver and gall-bladder, is good against gout and rheumatism. Works as an 'antibiotic', is anti-inflammatory and preservative.

Culinary use: as a sauce, with potatoes; a small amount may be mixed with apples and cream. Horse-radish is indispensable in pickling gherkins etc.

Hyssop (*Hyssopus officinalis*)

Medicinal effect: inhaled as a steam vapour, it acts quickly against colds in the head; promotes digestion.

Juniper (*Juniperus communis*)

Medicinal effect: acts as a diuretic and is therefore good for joint complaints; it is blood purifying, disinfects the urinary system and stimulates the appetite; it is generally disinfectant. Juniper is particularly good for diabetes.

Application: juniper is chewed raw and added to cooked food. *Caution:* Juniper can irritate the kidneys and should be used sparingly!

Culinary use: in *Sauerkraut*, in pickling gherkins and with beetroot; it may be added ground to sauces and whole to cream sauces and pickles such as pickled cabbage; juniper can be included in thick vegetable broths, and in soups.

Lavender (*Lavandula*)

Medicinal effect: has a beneficial action on the glands, is cholagogic (promoting the flow of bile to the intestine) and sedative.

Application: spirit of lavender may be sprinkled in bath water.

Domestic use: removes musty smells from old cupboards and discourages moths. Used in the linen-press.

Lovage (*Levisticum officinale*)
Medicinal effect: acts as a deodorant, carminative and improves perspiration; it has a favourable effect on the digestive system. Purifies the skin by internal action and cleanses the kidneys.
Cosmetic use: as an infusion, added to the bath for skin complaints.
Culinary use: used moderately but regularly in broths and soups and with heavy meals.

Marigold (*Calendula*)
Medicinal effect: known as a healing herb since the twelfth century and said to prevent cancer.
Application: the petals are used for ointments, in herbal teas and as an infusion for foot baths.
Culinary use: the yellow colouring matter is used instead of saffron; it may be added to soups, broths and sauces.

Marjoram (*Majorana hortensis*)
Medicinal effect: helpful against gastritis and colic; it is diaphoretic, diuretic and calming to the nerves.
Application: fresh or dried as a tisane.
Cosmetic use: in the evening baths.
Culinary use: in dumplings and potato dishes of all sorts, in stuffings and with vegetables; it should not be eaten by those with high blood pressure.

Mugwort (*Artemisia absinthum*)
Medicinal effect: promotes digestion, helps bladder trouble, improves the condition of the whole organism;it is particularly good against diabetes.
Application: given as a tea in cases of diarrhoea and stomach upset.
Culinary use: the buds are used in all so-called 'heavy' meals, with vegetables and fatty foods. Use freely in cases of diabetes.

Mustard (*Brassica nigra*)
Medicinal effect: it is healing, cleansing, disinfectant, regenerating and regulates the intestines. Mustard increases the activity of all the secretory organs, including the liver and gall-bladder.
Application: as mustard seed, powder, oil or plaster; the whole green plants are used when young.
Culinary use: seeds are taken with water for breakfast. Mustard powder is used to make a condiment for eggs etc., and is used as an ingredient in salad dressings. Mustard should always be at hand on the table! The seedlings are

used like cress seedlings, but surprisingly enough, they are milder.

Onion (*Allium*)
Medicinal effect: lowers the blood sugar more readily than perhaps any other pot herb; onion has a high vitamin C content and acts as an internal disinfectant, regulating the intestinal flora. Onion contains cardio-active substances and acts externally in skin complaints.
Application: raw, cooked and juiced.
Culinary use: a helpful flavouring in diabetic diets; use raw where possible, but in any case eat some onion daily. As a cooked vegetable, onions may be stuffed or mixed with green herbs etc.

Parsley (*Petroselinium crispum*)
Medicinal effect: regulates the digestion, contains an abundance of vitamins A, B and C; acts as a diuretic and an appetizer.
Application: the leaves and roots are used, but not the seeds!
Culinary use: parsley should be used regularly but not every day as it can prove irritating to the liver and kidneys. This herb goes well with nearly all vegetables and is added to salad dressings, uncooked foods, curd cheese, potatoes and stuffings.

Peppermint (Mentha piperita)
Medicinal effect: antispasmodic, anodyne, counteracts inflammation in the stomach.
Application: as a tea; as an oil in neuralgia and heartburn. Peppermint has an antiseptic action.
Culinary use: its use is limited, but peppermint goes well with vegetables and with blended foods.
Note: avoid using peppermint regularly over a long period of time as it can be harmful to the eyes.

Rosemary (*Rosemarinus officinalis*)
Medicinal effect: antispasmodic, improves the circulation, good for exhaustion, for the glands, and for high blood pressure; rosemary also increases the flow of bile.
Culinary use: used with indigestible stuffings of any kind.
Cosmetic use: in skin lotions, in baths, as a steam vapour and hair rinse.

Sage (*Salvia officinalis*)
Medicinal effect: purifies the blood, is good for the liver and gall-bladder;

beneficial in cases of gout, rheumatism, diabetes and laryngitis. Sage also reduces inflammation and acts as a deodorant.

Application: in the bath, and as an infusion for gargling; the fresh leaves are used as an application or first-aid dressing.

Cosmetic use: as a hair rinse and facial treatment when mixed with chamomile; acts as a deodorant and drives away moths.

Culinary use: may be added to sauces and dumplings; use freely in cases of diabetes.

Sorrel (*Rumex acetosa*)

Medicinal effect: blood purifying and appetizing; acts as an aid to digestion and has a high vitamin C content.

Culinary use: used in spring in vegetable soups and sauces; should be used with caution due to the oxalic acid content.

Spoonwort (*Cochlearia officinalis*)

Medicinal action: has a high vitamin C content and prevents scurvy.

Culinary use: may be added fresh to all uncooked foods; can also be used in stews.

Stinging-nettle (*Urtica dioica*)

Medicinal effect: diuretic, laxative, blood purifying, promotes the growth of hair (used as a lotion); it is body cleansing, good for the liver and gall-bladder and promotes lactation. According to an old herbal '... it is the richest herb and it has many right good properties...' Stinging nettles are a source of organic salts; they also help to reduce the level of sugar in the blood.

Application: use young leaves, fresh or dried. The seeds make a tea for cases of diarrhoea.

Culinary use: the young leaves may be added raw to all salads, vegetables, sauces and uncooked foods; nettles are especially good for a low-salt diet and may be used freely in cases of diabetes.

Cosmetic use: nettles make an excellent face pack when suitably prepared. (Do not apply while in stinging condition of course!)*

Summer savory (*Satureia hortensis*)

Medicinal effect: strengthens the nerves, liver and gall-bladder, regulates the appetite and digestion, strengthens the stomach.

*The words '...when suitably...of course!' have been added in the translation since the author does not say how to apply. *Tr.*

Application: the leaves are used, fresh or dried.
Culinary use: with all steamed vegetables, also with salads and other uncooked foods, with dumplings, sauces and stews.
Cosmetic use: savory is an excellent addition to the bath.

Tarragon (*Artemisia dracunculus*)
Medicinal effect: strengthens the stomach; is used for obstruction of the liver and in cases of jaundice. Tarragon is good against scurvy and rheumatism and helps to reduce the level of sugar in the blood.
Application: the leaves are used fresh; it may be added to vinegar and oil (in the bottle).
Culinary use: very helpful in a low-salt diet; it may be added to any salad or other type of uncooked food and used with mixed herbs, herb soups etc.

*Thyme (*Thymus vulgaris*)
Medicinal effect: the essential oil has a disinfectant action in coughs; it may be used as a tea in the treatment of worms.
Cosmetic use: it may be used in baths.
Culinary use: makes a very fine flavouring for peas and green beans, potato dishes, haricot beans, sauces, dumplings and soups.

*Valerian (*Valeriana officinalis*)
Medicinal effect: calmative and sleep-promoting.
Application: taken as an infusion (a tea), or in the form of an extract.
Caution: valerian should not be taken for any length of time (i.e. for more than two or three weeks on each occasion*).

*Wormwood (*Artemisia absinthium*)
Medicinal effect: benefits the glands, digestion, stomach, gall-bladder and circulation; wormwood corrects diseased or unhealthy conditions of the blood and may be used for cases of obesity.
Application: the infusion is taken in teaspoonful doses; do not drink when there is any bleeding.
Culinary use: wormwood is too bitter to make a suitable flavouring.

* Particular care is needed when using these herbs as an overdose is possible.

Useful Addresses

Chase Organics
Gibraltar House
Shepperton
Middlesex
TW17 8AQ

Henry Doubleday Research
    Association
Convent Lane
Bocking
Braintree
Essex
CM7 6RW

Organic Farm Supplies
Toke Place
Linton
Maidstone
Kent
ME17 4AP

Organic Growers Association
Aeron Park
Llangeitho
Dyfed
Wales

Soil Association
Walnut Tree Manor
Haughley
Stowmarket
Suffolk
IP14 3RS

Wyartt Seeds
Stone Cottage
Beyton
Bury St Edmunds
Suffolk
IP30 9AF

Index